Devising in Process examines the creative processes of eight theatre companies that make devising-based performances.

- The People Show
- Station House Opera
- Shunt
- The Red Room
- Faulty Optic Theatre of Animation
- Theatre O
- Gecko
- Third Angel

Authors were granted unusual access to the rehearsal room, enabling them to provide unique insights into how ideas evolve and develop, how strategies and methods are applied and how roles and relationships are structured. Covering a broad range of styles, the collection explores physical theatre, political theatre, puppetry, live art, new writing and performance with new technology.

Accessibly framed, the book includes a comprehensive introduction which highlights similarities and differences in approach, examines the impact of economic and cultural factors and explores how definitions of devised theatre are changing and developing. This eye-opening collection will be important reading for students and practitioners interested in exploring twenty-first-century devising processes.

ALEX MERMIKIDES is Senior Lecturer in Drama at Kingston University, where she leads the MA Devising Performance and the MA Playwriting, and teaches undergraduate students of drama, specialising in devising and writing for performance. She is a member of the Lightwork theatre company.

JACKIE SMART is Principal Lecturer in Drama at Kingston University, where she teaches devising, directing and physical theatre at undergraduate and postgraduate levels. She has devised and directed many productions both professionally and with students.

Devising in Process

Edited by

Alex Mermikides

and

Jackie Smart

palgrave
macmillan

First published 2010 by
PALGRAVE MACMILLAN

Palgrave Macmillan in the UK is an imprint of Macmillan Publishers Limited,
registered in England, company number 785998, of Houndmills, Basingstoke,
Hampshire RG21 6XS.

Palgrave Macmillan in the US is a division of St Martin's Press LLC,
175 Fifth Avenue, New York, NY 10010.

Palgrave Macmillan is the global academic imprint of the above companies
and has companies and representatives throughout the world.

Palgrave® and Macmillan® are registered trademarks in the United States,
the United Kingdom, Europe and other countries.

ISBN 978–0–230–57366–6   hardback
ISBN 978–0–230–57367–3   paperback

This book is printed on paper suitable for recycling and made from fully
managed and sustained forest sources. Logging, pulping and manufacturing
processes are expected to conform to the environmental regulations of the
country of origin.

A catalogue record for this book is available from the British Library.

A catalog record for this book is available from the Library of Congress.

10   9   8   7   6   5   4   3   2   1
19 18 17 16 15 14 13 12 11 10

Printed and bound in Great Britain by
CPI Antony Rowe, Chippenham and Eastbourne

Contents

List of Illustrations

Acknowledgements

Particular thanks must go to all the theatre companies and associated artists who so generously allowed access to their creative processes and contributed to the Devising in Process symposium. We would like to thank Shunt for hosting the symposium and Jane Milling and Deirdre Heddon for giving the keynote address. We are grateful to Adam Ainsworth at Kingston University for his comments on the manuscript and to Kate Haines and Jenni Burnell at Palgrave Macmillan for their help and guidance. The editors and publisher wish to thank Faulty Optic, Shunt and Third Angel for permission to reproduce images provided by the companies, and theatre O, Gecko and Station House Opera for permission to reproduce photographs taken by the authors in rehearsal.

Alex Mermikides would like to dedicate her part in this book to the memory of her father.

Notes on Contributors

Dr Alex Mermikides is a senior lecturer in drama at Kingston University, where she leads the MA course in Making Plays: Writing and Devising for the Stage. She is a member of Lightwork, a devising company specialising in the use of new technologies in theatre. Her research interests include contemporary theatre-making, writing for performance and twentieth and twenty-first-century British theatre.

Jackie Smart is a principal lecturer in drama at Kingston University. Her research interests lie in devising and physical theatre, and her published work includes studies of Random Dance Company, Forced Entertainment and Optic. With choreographer Lisa Cullen, Jackie founded Quisling, a company whose aim is to explore the relationships between different performance 'languages'.

Synne K. Behrndt lectures in performing arts at the University of Winchester. She is a practising dramaturg and has collaborated with performance companies in the UK and abroad. She is the co-author, with Dr Cathy Turner, of *Dramaturgy and Performance* (Palgrave Macmillan, 2007). Her areas of research and teaching include devising, cross-disciplinary practices and new dramaturgies.

Dr Helen Freshwater lectures at Birkbeck College, University of London, where she specialises in twentieth-century British theatre and contemporary performance. She is author of *Theatre Censorship in Britain: Silencing, Censure and Suppression* (Palgrave Macmillan, 2009) and *Theatre & Audience* (Palgrave Macmillan, 2009).

Dr Jem Kelly is a practice-led researcher specialising in multimedia, affective sound and phenomenology in performance, based at the University of Chichester. He is also Creative Director of Repeater Performance Theatre Co. As a musician, Jem composes for theatre and television advertising, and writes and performs songs with The Lotus Eaters.

Tim Moss leads the MA course in Writing for Performance at the University of Huddersfield and is a practising writer and script editor. He is on the board of management of IOU Theatre, having made nine performance works with them since 1993.

Philip Stanier leads the Performing Arts degree at the University of Winchester, and is artistic director of the Strange Names Collective (www.strangenamescollective.co.uk), which he founded in 2001. His research interests lie in live art and contemporary performance.

Dr Gareth White lectures in Applied Theatre at Central School of Speech and Drama, London and has also been an actor, director and facilitator, specialising in work with community groups and in educational settings. His recent publications address issues of agency and control in participatory theatre.

Introduction

This book offers eight case studies written by academic observers, each one following the process of making a devised show from start to finish. It is a resource for students and theatre-makers at every stage of their careers. It will also be useful to researchers of contemporary theatre, in terms both of providing documentation and analysis of devising processes and of offering models of how such processes might be written about.

In this respect the project negotiated some slippery issues. Few accounts of devising processes exist so we had few precedents on which to model our project. Of those that do exist, the majority are written by or from the perspective of the practitioners themselves. Practitioners writing about their own work can tend towards unintentional mystification, developing a shorthand form of expression where words and phrases have specific meanings, forged from shared training or experience, which can be impenetrable or misleading to the uninformed reader. There is a general sense that making the process too conscious can spoil the magic. As Guy Claxton puts it in *Navigating the Unknown*, 'there are a few creative people who fear that thinking about their creative process will make it fall apart' (in Bannerman, Sofaer and Watt, 2006, p. 60).

The other limitation within the existing studies of process is that they tend to look at solo processes, or at group processes as though they were solo processes: in other words, from the perspective of the director often to the exclusion of other participants. Devising, though, is a group activity and one that often contests the model of the singular creative artist. These factors underpinned our decision to ask academic observers to document and analyse these creative processes.

An 'outside' observer has the ability to see the process from multiple perspectives in a way that may be beyond any one artist within it.

It is essential to emphasise, though, that no writer could possibly see the whole of the process and that therefore the documentation and analysis presented in this book can only ever be partial and selective. In one case, the nature of the production itself prevented the writer from observing major aspects of its creation: Jem Kelly could not be in three countries at once when researching Station House Opera's *The Other Is You*, a telematic performance located (and rehearsed) in three different locations. More generally, though, writers had to make choices about which rehearsals they would attend and what aspects of process they would observe within those rehearsals.

It is also true to say, of course, that a great deal of creative work takes place where no one can see it – in the artists' own heads. The fact that devising is a group activity is helpful in this respect in that the work itself involves practitioners in articulating their private thoughts to each other, explaining their intentions and their reactions to ideas, improvisations and other proto-performances. One can also make use of various strategies for filling in the gaps, including interviews (formal and informal) with various company members, video records and, where companies are willing, reference to the artists' own notebooks or logs.

As the observations cannot be complete, neither can they be wholly objective. It is not a simple matter to maintain an outside stance when sitting in on creative activity. In part this is because many of the companies were not happy to have someone in the rehearsal room who did not participate in some way, whether by joining in warm-ups or by offering opinions on what was taking place in front of them. In part it is because observers bring into the rehearsal room their own set of beliefs and experiences, which will inevitably affect how they look and listen and what they see and hear. As writers we cannot help but 'translate' what we observe, leaving much out, deciding on an order, choosing our words and, of course, making our own interpretation of the evidence. What an academic writer can bring is a sense of the historical, methodological and critical contexts within which to locate the process s/he observes. Moreover, our choice to focus each chapter on the creation of a single show offers, we feel, the best opportunity to identify and examine the actual strategies and techniques employed by devising companies when making their work. In particular, we asked our writers to look at how the context of a specific show determines both which strategies and techniques are used and how.

Perhaps the most difficult question presented by this exercise concerns the selection of companies and projects to feature in this volume. Our concern has been to try to represent the great diversity of contemporary practice by selecting companies whose work covers a wide range of approaches and contexts. In comparing and contrasting these, we can highlight elements of process and draw out principles that a number of companies have in common, and we can also look at how these companies stand in relation to the history of devising by considering their influences and links. We do not attempt to construct any singular definition of devising or any set of definitions of strands of devising and we do not, and could not within one volume, aim to offer an exhaustive picture of devising today.

In *Devising Performance* (2006) Heddon and Milling recognise that the 'danger of any book of this sort is that, through the inclusion of particular examples, those companies become, by default, canonical' – even if they are not the only, or 'the most important', devising companies (p. 26). Elaborating on this point in the symposium we held while the research was underway, they asked 'Who gets placed in the archive? Who gets written about? Who is in the book?'[1] One implication of their questions is that those whose work gets documented, especially those whose work gets documented by academics, are those whose work will survive. In selecting particular companies we are indicating that we, as academics, value their work and think it representative of the wider devised practice of the current moment. We are pleased to be bringing the work of important companies to greater public attention but we are also aware that in doing so we are leaving out many more.

We chose to focus primarily on UK-based companies, partly because we felt that their processes are currently under-represented within critical texts and partly because we wanted to introduce new audiences to the wide range of excellent work currently taking place in Britain. The last ten years in the UK have produced a plethora of highly creative devising-based companies but, until recently, much critical and analytical material has focused on a few older, more established groups, for example DV8, Forced Entertainment and Complicite. With this book we wanted to represent a wider range and also to identify those companies we feel are likely to be the influences of the future, as inspirational to current generations of students as those listed above were to our generation. Most of our featured companies regularly tour nationally and internationally; many enjoy considerable international success and boast significant reputations in continental Europe, performing regularly on the European theatre festival circuit as well as further afield. Although all the companies that feature here are respected in the field and have achieved critical acclaim, some have been going a lot longer than others and all are at different stages of their careers. The People

Show, founded in 1966, is not just the 'oldest' company in the book, but also the longest-running in the UK, while the production documented here of our 'youngest' company, Gecko, is only its third.

In selecting these companies, then, we are aware that they could be seen as representing 'devising today'. This is problematic, given both the range of practices encompassed by the term and the fact that devising is at an interesting and fluid point of its history. While it was once an alternative and radical form of theatre-making, devising is now recognised as one of the major methodologies through which leading contemporary companies and practitioners create innovative work on an international scale: DV8, Complicite, Forced Entertainment, Robert Lepage, Goat Island, the Wooster Group and Pina Bausch are some of the best-known names in a growing canon of practitioners whose international reputation regularly fills auditoria of main houses and the festival circuit. The extent of the infiltration of devising methods into mainstream professional practice is greater than we might at first suppose: Harvie and Lavender, in their forthcoming book *Making Contemporary Theatre: International Rehearsal Processes*, discovered that most of their selected practitioners and companies – all major figures in terms of defining cutting edge performance on the international scale – used some form of devising. In the Introduction, the editors state that:

> The popularity of devising in the work represented here reflects its move within theatre-making from a fairly marginal position in the 1970s to one of significant disciplinary and institutional orthodoxy in the first decade of the twenty-first century.
>
> (Harvie and Lavender, 2010)

It might seem strange to use the term 'orthodoxy' in relation to devising, which started out as a counter-cultural practice populated by iconoclastic practitioners acting in resistance to traditional forms and theatre conventions. The term was also used, though, by Deirdre Heddon and Jane Milling in their keynote address at our symposium, where they asked:

> Has devising in fact now become a new orthodoxy? Has the presence of it as part of a company's or practitioner's repertoire become a necessary marker of cutting edge performance? Or is it the inevitable result of an increasingly active interdisciplinary work that companies are both seeking out or being encouraged into?

One result of this 'mainstreaming' of devising is that many of the original assumptions of devising are in flux – a point that Alison Oddey made as far back as 1994 in her seminal text, *Devising Theatre: A Practical and Theoretical Handbook*. Making a comparison with the early years of devising in the 1970s she writes: 'in the cultural climate of the 1990s the term "devising" has less radical implications, placing greater emphasis on skill sharing, specific roles, increasing division of responsibilities ... and more hierarchical group structures' (1994, p. 9). The prevalence of devising today and its presence in 'institutional' venues such as the National Theatre and the Barbican surely mean that it can no longer be seen as either radical or resistant. If it is now an orthodoxy, what are the current assumptions about it? If earlier models of devising process represented collaboration as an alternative to the hierarchy of the director's theatre, is contemporary devising still defined by its collaborative nature and, if so, what kinds of collaboration are employed? Do established traditions of devising still have an influence? What kinds of relationship now exist between visual, physical, verbal and textual elements of performance? By looking at what companies actually do in the rehearsal room we can begin to address such questions. However, we are not aiming to give any singular answers to them but rather, by selecting a range of companies, we seek to illustrate the variety of responses that different companies come up with across the multiplicity of contexts within which they operate.

As both Heddon and Milling (2006) and Govan, Nicholson and Normington (2007) emphasise, devising today encompasses a number of contexts, traditions, lineages and ideologies which have become intertwined. Disentangling the various genealogies is no small task and a thorough historical account of these is beyond the scope of this Introduction. However, it is important to consider the extent to which our featured companies represent some of the major strands within current devising practice and the lineages that link their work to earlier traditions. We are aware that a collection of this scope cannot hope to represent every strand of devising practice. Of the streams of practice that we are unable to cover in this volume, by far the most prevalent is applied theatre, although The Red Room draws on the principles of this form. Other significant types of devising that are not represented here include site-specific work such that of Punchdrunk and Grid Iron, and task and game-based work such as that of Reckless Sleepers and Blast Theory.

What the existing strands might be is not universally agreed, though Heddon and Milling, and Govan, Nicholson and Normington both recognise several key areas. We use these as a starting point for the following discussion of postmodern performance, live art, performance art and visual theatre; physical performance; and political and applied theatre. This is something we do with several caveats. We are aware that there is no universal agreement about exactly where the lines of distinction between these strands and traditions lie. We must also stress that not every company fits neatly into one of these categories; for example Station House Opera might be defined as postmodern performance, as visual theatre or as representative of the growing strand of technology-driven or multi/mixed media performance – or even, as Julian Maynard Smith suggested in a conversation with the editors, something outside theatre altogether.

As Maynard Smith's comment suggests, practitioners themselves will often resist the 'labelling' that academics and critics impose upon them. Even on the rare occasion that a company invents its own category, as when DV8's Lloyd Newson coined the term 'physical theatre', the members might subsequently retract or problematise their own term. As Heddon and Milling suggest, 'the practices, companies, aims, forms, and even personnel blur' (p. 27), and their caution against attempting to create clear-cut categories of devising practice is uppermost in our minds even as we recognise the value of mapping out common practices, artistic and ideological policies and influences among our featured companies.

Postmodern performance, live art, performance art and visual theatre

Heddon and Milling describe postmodern performance as a form that responds to a particular set of theoretical discourses that emerged in the 1970s and 1980s, 'variously described as post-structuralist, postmodernist or post-colonial' (p. 190) that challenged 'the status of (or belief in) "grand narratives" and of appeals to "universal truths"' (p. 191). They discuss how Forced Entertainment, The Special Guests and Third Angel (from the UK) and Goat Island and the Wooster Group (from the United States) use collaborative devising processes to match these conceptual concerns. Devising in this context, they say, contests the authority of text and of the individual creative artist – and, by implication, any suggestion of a singular 'truth'. It allows for the creation of work in which narrative is continually disrupted and which draws attention to its own constructed-ness in order to 'make transparent the constructed narrative status of our (and its) interpretations/re-presentations of the world' (p. 191). The post-structuralist aspect in particular challenges modernist processes of meaning-making, so that the work becomes an escape from representation and closed fictional frames (Peggy Phelan defines this as 'representation without representation' (1992, p. 3)) and throws the onus of making sense of the work onto the audience member.

This radicalising of the audience's role has, since around the 1980s, coalesced into a preoccupation with 'liveness' and, with this, an emphasis on the 'reality' of audience, performer and their meeting in real time. For this reason the term 'live art' has become synonymous with postmodern performance (in the UK at least). As the term suggests, there is an association with visual art practices, though Amelia Jones' survey of crossovers between visual arts and performance identifies live art's origins as when 'performance art proper split off from the visual arts, aligning itself with theatre' (2002, p. 36). As the 'theatre' arm of performance art, live art quickly established its own tradition.

Of our featured companies, Third Angel and Station House Opera most clearly represent this strand of current practice. In the various showings that constitute Third Angel's *9 Billion Miles from Home*, and in Station House Opera's *The Other is You*, postmodern concerns are manifested in a deconstruction of the concept of fiction. The 'ritual' that represents the culmination of *9 Billion Miles* is not representational. It presents itself for what it is: a series of tasks performed in front of the audience. Although some of the scenarios that are created by the performers in *The Other is You* may suggest relationships, exchanges and emotional journeys, the foregrounding of the technology, our awareness that we are watching a series of prescribed movements responding to camera cues constantly subverts our instinct to make a 'story'. Thus, both performances reject 'character': Third Angel performers Alex Kelly and Gillian Lees play 'themselves'; in Station House Opera, performers become what Jem Kelly describes as 'personae'. In both cases, the performances expose their own constructed-ness.

While Third Angel and Station House Opera typify the live art tradition, the People Show, Shunt and, perhaps less definitively, Faulty Optic illustrate that of performance art. Performance art grew out of visual art movements of the 1950s in response to conceptual discourses that challenged established practices and world-views. These included action painting, conceptual art and happenings, but performance art found its form in the alternative theatre movement of the 1960s and 1970s as what Kershaw describes as 'carnivalesque' theatre that 'challenged the dominant ideologies through the production of alternative pleasures' (1999, p. 40). He lists as examples the People Show, Welfare State International (the only other survivor from this period), Exploding

Galaxy, Mark Boyle's Sensual Laboratory and John Bull Puncture Repair Kit, recognising their taste for symbolic, synaesthetic, multi-layered and hallucinogenic performance and a desire to 'shock the audience into a new kind of "expanded" liberated consciousness' (p. 71). Blurring boundaries between disciplines (theatre and art in particular) and between 'high' and 'low' art, performance art produced work with a 'punk aesthetic' (Goldberg, 2001, p. 181) that juxtaposed seemingly incompatible forms, styles and objects in a way that alludes to the way in which the technique of 'cut up' and found objects were employed by the Dadaists and their followers.

In some cases, the blurring of disciplinary boundaries also means an expansion of the typical range of theatrical languages and elements. The People Show states as its policy a commitment to creating 'multi-disciplinary, multi-media live theatre' through a process that 'draws together a diverse range of practitioners into the mix'.[2] Shunt is unusual in that its members are too young to have experienced the movement first-hand, but, as discussed in Alex Mermikides' chapter, their approach and aesthetic clearly align them to this tradition – and the People Show's policy could equally describe the way in which Shunt sets up a structure in which creative friction between members' various interests and skills translate into a collage-form of performance.

Although, like these companies, Faulty Optic's work also blurs the disciplinary boundaries between theatre and art, the company sits less comfortably within this category. Its work is less radical in its challenge to conventional narrative forms (though not by any means traditional in its story-telling techniques). Its defining feature – the unique use of puppetry and animation – aligns Faulty Optic with companies such as Improbable Theatre, Horse and Bamboo, Forkbeard Fantasy, Hesitate and Demonstrate, IOU and Welfare State, which often use found or made objects in place of or alongside the performer and always regard the scenographic aspect as a dominant language of performance. This strand of practice might be described as visual theatre, though the term seems to have fallen out of common usage in recent years since its popularity in the 1980s (Heddon and Milling use the slightly more contemporary 'visual performance'). Like performance art, visual theatre tends to emerge from fine art and is often practised by art-school graduates. If there is a distinction to be made from performance art 'proper' (and this is arguable given that, for example, the People Show has been cited as part of this tradition), it is in its less radical stance. Like physical theatre, visual theatre represents a challenge to the dominance of the text and the spoken word, but its expressionistic focus on inner states, atmosphere and emotion makes it ultimately more modernist than postmodern.

Physical theatre

In *Physical Theatres: A Critical Introduction* (2007) Murray and Keefe use the term 'physical theatres/the physical in theatre' both to indicate the plurality of physical modes of performance and to hint at the absorption into theatre generally of somatic concerns and practices once seen as experimental and decidedly non-establishment. Although 'ruthlessly insistent' on using the plural term 'with all its consequent implications for suggesting a diversity of forms built from different roots and technical traditions' (p. 4), they identify a shared principle within the various strands of historical influence on contemporary physical performance, suggesting that '"physical theatre" ... traces its origins in our contemporary sense to those ideologies and manifestos which sought to reverse a dualism and hierarchy of word over body' (p. 7). In her important essay 'Altered States and Subliminal Spaces: Charting the Road Towards a Physical Theatre' Ana Sanchez-Colberg considers the development of physical and dance theatres in terms of post-structural concerns with language, arguing that a motivating factor in the development of movement-based theatre forms has been:

> a progressive devaluation of language ... based on ... a mistrust of ... a language which aims to articulate, and thus contain, universal truths without questioning the material practices which gave rise to that language.
>
> (Sanchez-Colberg, 1996, p. 41)

This mistrust of language, though, should not be understood as a simple rejection of the word or the text. Artaud, Grotowski and Meyerhold, while each espousing the belief that the body was the locus of a deeper, more primal truth than language, all worked with playtexts. What they rejected was the authority of the word and, by extension, of the playwright. These practitioners sought plays which addressed what they considered to be universal human concerns, yet treated the playtext as a resource which could be cut up, interrogated, its 'authorial' meaning challenged through juxtaposition with image, action, gesture and vocal delivery. theatre O's choice and 're-interpretation' of Dostoevsky's classic text, *The Brothers Karamazov*, clearly owes something to such approaches in terms both of the grand themes of the original and the liberties the company feels entitled to take with it (although, as Helen Freshwater reveals in Chapter 6 of this book, the text does not entirely lose its 'authority').[3]

Dancers meanwhile, influenced by the American postmodern and British new dance movements, have embraced physical theatre as a means of challenging conventional notions of what constitutes dance and disrupting the 'languages' of codified dance techniques, often by including spoken text within their work. In Germany, Pina Bausch's influential 'Tanztheater' has dealt with embodied politics, especially gender politics, interrogating the body and physical behaviours as sites of cultural inscription. This kind of physical theatre, exemplified in Britain by DV8 and, more recently, Frantic Assembly 'was formed out of a desire to enable the development of the dancer as a creative artist with something to say' (Chamberlain and Yarrow, 2002, p. 7) and the rejection of choreographer-dominated forms in order to emphasise the creative autonomy of the dancer in the process. Specifically dance-based physical theatre is not represented in our book, although its influence can be seen in Gecko's focus on the emotional and psychic landscape of the individual and their investigation in *The Arab and The Jew* of how their cultural inheritances impact upon their bodies and relationships. The images and actions created in the piece are deliberately suggestive of more than one meaning, refusing to 'contain' any pre-existing notion of 'universal truths' but rather an ambiguous and highly personal truth.

Gecko and theatre O to different degrees both exemplify Dymphna Callery's definition of physical theatre as a style that involves the 'actor-as-creator rather than the actor-as-interpreter' (2001, p. 5). Callery also suggests that physical theatre is a form in which 'working process is collaborative' (p. 5) – a belief that is widespread. Complicite (one of the best known companies emerging from this tradition), for example, states that 'what is essential is collaboration. A collaboration between individuals to establish an ensemble with a common physical and imaginative language.'[4] It is this collaborative agenda, especially the creative emancipation of the performer in rejection of the written text, which makes physical theatre a form that is 'ideally suited to devising companies' (Lamden, 2000, p. 4), even though, historically, physical theatre was not necessarily devised.

These aspects of contemporary physical theatre might be attributed, at least in part, to the teaching (and pedagogical practices) of the Lecoq school in Paris: 'Lecoq's emphasis on provoking the actor's imagination and creativity is a means of freeing actors from the "tyranny of text" in order to create their own scenarios' (Chamberlain and Yarrow, 2002, p. 4).

The approach was popularised in the 1980s by a generation of companies who had spent their year in Paris 'doing Lecoq', most notably Théâtre de Complicité (now Complicite), whose first performance at the National Theatre in 1992, *The Street of Crocodiles*, 'marked the legitimisation ... of a process of theatre-making that has its roots in the workshop rather than written text' (Lavender, 1999, p. 181). The influence of Lecoq on our featured companies is evident: Joseph Alford and Carolina Valdes of theatre O met at Lecoq while Amit Lahav and Al Nedjari from Gecko have worked with people who have incorporated Lecoq techniques into their own practice (David Glass and Steven Berkoff).

Political and applied theatre

This notion of emancipating the practitioner (most usually the performer) from the 'tyranny' inherent in 'mainstream' practices was an ideal of the explicitly left-wing theatre collectives of the 1970s, a highly influential, if short-lived, area of practice. Political theatre as a *devised* form was particularly vulnerable to the funding cuts of the late 1970s (more so than the political dramatists who were also making their mark at the time) but for a brief period government subsidy of the arts (whether through the Arts Council or the dole) allowed a flourishing of left-wing, activist companies such as 'Red Ladder, Joint Stock, Welfare State International, 7:84, Avon Touring, Belt and Braces, Women's Theatre Group, Monstrous Regiment and Gay Sweatshop' (Goodman, 1993, pp. 52–3). Acting on the principle that 'the relations of production within the group should reflect its politics and provide a model for the organization of society as a whole' (p. 55), many of these companies worked in ways that rejected the authority of the director and the writer, doing away with hierarchical and patriarchal models and, in their most extreme forms, role distinctions. Thus:

> the collective approach to work breaks down the boundaries between the different areas of production and, consequently, the status or importance traditionally attached to certain roles. Ideally, everyone has a say, everyone shares both the challenging/exciting and the tedious aspects of the work, everyone is happy and fulfilled.
>
> (p. 91)

Goodman's term 'ideally' is significant: her discussion of feminist collective companies suggests that reality rarely lived up to the ideal, particularly because, as Clare Grove argues in a discussion cited by Goodman (1991), collective approaches tended to blunt the political and dramatic effectiveness of the work produced. What is significant though is that, irrespective of methodological issues, the collective has had a seminal influence on subsequent practice. Even though, as Heddon and Milling acknowledge (p. 5), there has been a return to hierarchical structure, a trace of the principle of collectivism remains in the ideology of contemporary devising companies, irrespective of their political orientation. It underlies their commitment to 'collaborative' creative approaches and their challenge to the authority of the playwright and the director. All our featured companies honour the principle of anti-hierarchal organisational structure, even if they are not all equally explicit in their commitment to, and are variously successful in their realisation of, these principles.

It is surprising then that, although it is the most explicitly political of our featured companies and an example of issue-based performance that is relatively rare now, The Red Room is perhaps the furthest from the collective structure: Topher Campbell's authority as a director and Fin Kennedy's work as the playwright make for a process that has more in common with the orthodox script-led practices that the collective sought to challenge. Yet the inclusion of a writer into the collective group has its precedent in the practices of Joint Stock, Monstrous Regiment and the Women's Theatre Group as it evolved into Sphinx, companies which began as collective devising companies but fairly quickly decided to establish 'a collective relationship with a writer' (Hanna, 1991, p. xxxiii). It is significant that two of the three surviving companies from Goodman's list have become new writing companies –something that suggests that survival, in the particular economical and political climate, might require a closer approximation to established working practices.

Having located our featured companies within the wider historical and contemporary context, we will now go on to draw together some of the observations made in the process of creating this book that might usefully inform further characterisations of devising. Two themes struck us as particularly significant. Firstly, we will look at how notions of collaboration and authorship play out in the structures and roles adopted by different companies. As previously discussed, one of the markers of devising's new position as an 'orthodoxy' has been to challenge its perhaps mythical status as an inherently anti-hierarchical form; the discussion that follows outlines some of the implications of this. We will then close this Introduction by mapping out common practices across our featured companies in terms of key stages of the devising processes. We do not do this in order to suggest any sort of prescriptive model of the devising process. As practitioners ourselves, we are aware that there is something of a slippage between the neatly framed, somewhat 'idealised' methods we offer our students in class and the messy realities of making a show. In the world of professional theatre practice, of course, this is even more of an issue. Companies have all sorts of factors to deal with beyond the show itself. In the section below, we explore the relationship such factors have with the aesthetic concerns of practitioners.

Company structures and roles

The ways in which companies structure themselves are influenced by pragmatic and economic as well as artistic concerns: what strand of the funding hierarchy they fit into (small, medium or large scale) and whether they are funded on a core or project basis; their relationships with venues and/or those who have commissioned a given project; where they rehearse and perform and whether they have a 'home' base. These factors in turn impact upon key aspects of the creative process such as how many people a project involves, the roles those people take on and the time available for rehearsals.

A comparison between the structure of the oldest and newest companies included in this volume sheds light on how UK arts funding mechanisms impact over time on working methods. The People Show, founded in 1966, is a registered charity with core funding from the Arts Council. Core funding does not imply that companies do not need to seek financial support from elsewhere – venues, festivals, sponsors and additional project-based funding from the Arts Council – but it does enable some, including the People Show, to maintain a permanent administrative team and a home base (as with People Show Studios in East London). This location provides office, rehearsal and performance space as well as extra revenue streams from running workshops and hiring out space to other practitioners. As is common practice amongst performance practitioners at all levels of funding, the company also maintains an educational programme from which it receives an income.

The People Show is best described as a loose collective. Of the five founder members only one remains in the current group of seven artists who form the company's core. Others artists are invited to contribute to specific projects, some drawn from the extensive network of relationships the company has formed over its long existence and some new to the People Show. None of the People Show artists work exclusively for the People Show; in fact all the artists, including the core members, are employed on a project-by-project basis. As Synne Behrndt explains in Chapter 1, 'the company's ethos of process and performance is currently reflected in their organisational structure where instead of an artistic director a steering group consults with a wide network of People Show associate artists on future projects and planning.' The company explains its creative philosophy on its website:

> Our non-autocratic ethos is still as relevant today as it was at the inception of the company, and, in order to retain our cutting edge and innovative style of inquiry, we maintain a balance of creative input between the longer-standing members of the company and new artists.[5]

The People Show is in the unusual position of being an established but still decidedly non-mainstream company; unlike Complicite or Kneehigh, you will not see the People Show performing on the main stages of, for instance, the National Theatre or the Barbican. The company has achieved a level of stability thanks to its home base and core funding which enables it to maintain an administrative team but it has resisted incorporation into any kind of traditional theatre 'system', preferring to retain its independent vision and the creative freedom rooted in its experimental, art-based heritage. To this end, it is important to the company not to become defined creatively by the ideas of any one person or group of people who contribute to every show.

Unlike the People Show, Gecko, formed in 2001, is not in receipt of core funding. Nor did the company, at the time of writing, have a permanent home base (although it has since moved to Ipswich to become company in residence at the New Wolsey Theatre). *The Arab and The Jew* gained project-based Arts Council funding and further financial support, often 'in kind', from eight different small to middle-scale venues around the country. 'In-kind' support means that venues provide some rehearsal space and access to technical and administrative resources rather than specific amounts of actual cash. One consequence of this funding pattern for Gecko was that the creative process and rehearsals of the production took place at different locations in intermittent blocks of time, interrupted by other revenue-raising activities. Some of these were related to the artistic work of the company – like the People Show, Gecko offers workshops for schools, colleges and universities – and some purely to earning a living. An extended and fragmented process such as this makes it difficult to have a large cast because such a set-up makes it hard for actors to accept other work. This influenced Amit Lahav and Allel Nedjari's decision to work as a pair on this production, although there were also creative reasons for this.

The Arab and The Jew was produced by Fuel, a production company which supports a number of different theatre companies and artists, assisting with funding applications, negotiating relationships with venues and doing some marketing and administration. It is worth mentioning Fuel because, along with Arts Admin, it has played a vital role in providing support and encouragement for emerging artists. However the fact that neither the company nor the production was Fuel's sole focus meant that the organisational aspects of creating the production were fragmented, leaving gaps that the creative team had to fill. This also applied to the technical side of the production. The production manager for *The Arab and The Jew* was employed by Fuel, and therefore only available to Gecko for limited and specific periods, while the Arts Council's initial rejection of the funding application resulted in changes to design and to technical personnel, whom Gecko could not afford to retain while they re-applied. In fact, in a year when the Arts Council were making quite sweeping cuts, the original plans of several companies had to change. Budget cuts meant that the co-artistic director of theatre O, Joseph Alford, reversed his original decision not to perform in *Delirium*, while Julian Maynard Smith explains in Kelly's chapter on Station House Opera that the length of the creative process was curtailed by the limited finances available (other companies we approached had had to cancel projects altogether).

The stability of a company then, which is determined to a large extent by its funding situation, inevitably impacts on its structure. Louise Blackwell of Fuel suggests that, although essential to new and emerging artists, project-based funding is 'an impossible way to exist over time'.[6] While the People Show continues to resist incorporation into the mainstream, its core funding and home base facilitate a collective ethos which it is much more difficult for less-established companies to achieve. Project-based funding, the basis on which many small to medium-scale companies operate, mitigates against administrative cohesion and impacts upon the availability of creative and technical personnel.

Another external factor that can shape company structures and approaches to collaboration is whether a project has been commissioned and by whom. Some commissioners take a very hands-off approach; for instance Chelsea Theatre, which commissioned Third Angel to create *9 Billion Miles from Home*, required only that the company give a work-in-progress performance in their 'Sacred' season of Live Art.

Other commissioners have much greater control and impact. Tim Moss explains that Faulty Optic normally choose to collaborate with people whose work they know well, and that ideas emerge 'organically' through conversation and the sharing of ideas. *Dead Wedding*, though, was commissioned by Opera North and the Manchester International Festival, whose terms were that the piece should be a collaboration between the company and a composer/musician, and that the commissioners should have approval over the choice of composer. The company's first choice was rejected and the composer who eventually became their collaborator chose to work in a very different way from the company's usual method. She did not sit in on rehearsals, composing in response to the work Faulty Optic was producing; instead the company sent her a kind of score with timings and 'emotional temperatures' for each scene. Because they had not created all the scenes at this point, the effect was to make the length of the music an essential shaping factor as well as making the collaborative process less immediate and interactive than had previously been the case.

Funding has an obvious impact on how many people a company can afford to maintain as a core team. One resolution to this economic issue is the employment of the core-and-pool structure, described by Katie Mitchell, referring to Théâtre de Complicité, as 'a constellation of performers whom they draw on for different productions' (1999, p. 71). This structure is common to many British theatre companies where there is a small permanent core, usually made up of founder members, almost always including an artistic director. Individual projects may bring together a larger number of participants and these will normally be people to whom the company returns again and again. As Freshwater demonstrates in her chapter on theatre O, one of the benefits of this structure is that the participants in a process share an aesthetic and/or methodological 'language' even though they do not always work together. Another advantage is that the structure can satisfy a desire for novelty both in the process (the fresh input of new collaborators) and in the project (so that each new production has a different size and composition of cast appropriate to the form and content of the show). Ironically, given that devising is often seen as a process that empowers the performer to give creative input, it is frequently performers who constitute the 'pool' and who are therefore often the newcomers, and thus less able to assert authorship, in a particular process.

Half the companies in this book are structured around a core of two. Faulty Optic is Gavin Glover and Liz Walker, Third Angel is Alex Kelly and Rachael Walton, theatre O is Joseph Alford and Carolina Valdes, and Gecko at the time of writing was Amit Lahav and Allel Nedjari (although Nedjari has since departed from the company). We have come to understand the popularity of working as a pair as a resolution of two conflicting factors: the desire on the one hand for group structures that enable collaboration and to some degree resist sole directorial authority, and on the other, the economic difficulty of continuously sustaining a large group of people. It is interesting how many devising companies start off as a larger core which over time reduces itself to two members or even one artistic director. For example, Complicite, which was founded as Théâtre de Complicité by Annabel Arden, Marcello Magni and Simon McBurney, is now led by McBurney (the name change, in 1999, coincided with this shift in structure).

This brings us to a consideration of the internal structures of the companies examined here, the different roles company members take on and the relationships these construct. We are particularly interested in the ways in which such roles and relationships shed light upon key concepts related to devising such as collaboration, company identity, ownership and authority.

An instructive comparison can be made between Shunt, Third Angel and Station House Opera, companies that share some lines of postmodern heritage. None of them performs on the conventional theatre circuit: Third Angel has established itself within universities and more experimental arts centres, producing film and installation as well as theatre performance; Station House Opera does a lot of work at arts festivals in Britain and internationally; and Shunt has created its own very idiosyncratic performance space, which is also a members' bar. These alternatives to conventional theatre spaces enable these companies to escape, to some degree, some of the strictures of conventional theatre schedules. Station House Opera is led by a single artistic director and Third Angel by a pair, while Shunt operates as a collective of ten artists.

Of these three, Third Angel perhaps best fits existing assumptions about how a devising company is structured in that there is no director or writer and all roles are shared. Kelly and Walton work both separately and together under the company banner. While the starting point for *9 Billion Miles from Home* arose out of a particular interest of Kelly's in the *Voyager 2* spacecraft, he had no desire to retain 'ownership' over his idea. In Phil Stanier's account of the process, Kelly and Walton almost always express themselves as 'we', conveying a sense of shared investment in the ideas and processes they discuss.

Central to this sense of shared investment is the fact that the company's process draws on autobiography and the emotional responses of each participant in a piece to the material explored, meaning that the discovery of different, perhaps conflicting, perspectives on the theme or subject matter is a positive benefit rather than a problem. Another factor is that Kelly and Walton both have skills and interest in the various activities their process demands, skills they also seek in their collaborators when working on larger pieces: researching, writing, making objects, improvisation and performing. The process of making *9 Billion Miles from Home,* as described by Stanier, was characterised by experimentation, discussion and debate, with the final product emerging from a cyclical voyage of discovery with detours down interesting tracks, rather than a controlled journey directed towards a known destination. Even between two people who know each other well and have worked together over a long period, though, this level of collaborative openness takes time – like Gecko's *The Arab and The Jew,* the total creative process took more than a year. Paradoxically, time is often less available to more conventionally 'successful' companies who must negotiate space and time with venues that operate according to commercial imperatives, though all companies have to make difficult choices as to how best to spend their finite funds.

The choice made by Julian Maynard Smith, artistic director of Station House Opera, was to sacrifice time for collaborative play in favour of technological experimentation. *The Other is You* combined simultaneous performances in three countries into a screen triptych in front of which the live actors in each location played out their scenes. Jem Kelly suggests that the performance was 'shaped to some extent autocratically'. Although the project's multi-country location required three directors, Julian Maynard Smith was the originator of the idea, which developed out of his previous productions, and he hired the other directors to work under his company name. The directors met for an exchange of ideas before rehearsals began but time pressures limited this kind of creative sharing. Maynard Smith also had responsibility for the vast amount of planning and preparation needed for this highly technical production, which placed him in a position of knowledge and authority from the beginning. Within this quite hierarchical structure there was room for creative input from the other directors, who worked uninterrupted with their respective casts in the mornings and each developed differing approaches and areas of focus, but fewer opportunities for creative contributions from the performers. The need for precision created by the technical demands of *The Other Is You* also limited the scope of what they could do. It was in the afternoons, when the three sets of contributors 'met' online, that Maynard Smith's authority came into play because he retained overall control of the combined image in order to create visual cohesion in the performances. Kelly suggests that Maynard Smith played the role of an *auteur* and we can see that this derives from a complicated mixture of personality, company history, time constraints and technical complexity.

Shunt is a company which has found ways to directly address the traps and difficulties which lie within the realm of authority as it is played out through company structure. Members of Shunt call them-selves artists in order to avoid the demarcation of roles traditionally associated with theatre production (director, actor, designer and so on). It is revealing though, that in the 'big shows' at least, the artists tend to stick relatively closely to their area of specialist knowledge, taking responsibility for particular elements on a regular basis. These roles are not credited on publicity material and there is flexibility and negotia-tion between them. It is significant that defined areas of responsibility only emerge at a later stage of the process where, in particular, the directorial role becomes important in bringing some cohesiveness to the individual work different company members have been doing. Thus all the Shunt artists are 'authors' in the sense of having a high level of creative input but an individual director has final responsibility for creating a coherent (though not necessarily unified) vision. The *Shunt Lounge* takes this flexibility of roles further by allowing individual art-ists freedom to create and perform their own work without attempting to make these separate creations cohere into a single piece. The *Lounge* also shares out directorial responsibilities as the artists take it in turns to curate it.

The relationship between collaboration and authority, then, plays out in various ways within different companies and is shaped by many factors. Third Angel's open and exploratory approach both arises out of and contributes to the 'multi-stranded' nature of its work, as does Shunt's. It is easier for a company of two to retain a shared vision and shared responsibility for all roles throughout the process, though, than it is for a collective of ten. Even within Shunt's fragmentary, non-linear productions it is necessary for a director to take on the task of shaping, but Shunt continues to consciously seek innovative ways of facilitating a sense of shared ownership and joint responsibility. Julian Maynard Smith's more authoritarian directorial approach is a response, in some degree, to the technical demands of the particular project described, as well as to time constraints, but it also has to do with Maynard Smith's role as sole artistic director and the only constant across all this long-standing company's works.

These questions of authority and creative ownership become still more complex when a devising company chooses to work with a playwright, as did two of the companies in this book: theatre O, who collaborated with playwright Enda Walsh on an adaptation of Dostoyevsky's *The Brothers Karamazov*; and The Red Room, whose piece, *Unstated*, was written by Fin Kennedy. The distinction conventionally made between writing and devising is somewhat misleading. Collaborations between writers and devisers have in fact been taking place since the 1960s and today there is something of a fashion for companies known for devising to undertake collaborations with writers, as, for example, Frantic Assembly did with Mark Ravenhill in their production *Pool No Water* (2006), or for writers to use devising as a tool within their process, as Anthony Neilson has done (see Reid, 2007). In both cases documented in this book, what emerges clearly is that the central collaboration took place between writer and director. This does not mean that the performers had no creative input but it was certainly more contained and controlled than that of most of the other projects documented.

Gareth White explains that *Unstated* was a new departure for The Red Room, who have previously produced plays from existing scripts, so it is not altogether surprising that their company structure reflects more traditional models. On the other hand, Fin Kennedy's previous experience of the company (he had developed his work through The Red Room's writers' group) meant that his approach as playwright was more collaborative than would normally be the case in conventional writers' theatre, sitting in on rehearsals for example. White describes the model adopted by The Red Room as involving 'interlocking circles of collaboration', the first of which took place within an extended period of research which included consultation with a 'reference group' made up of groups and individuals with authoritative knowledge about the subject matter of the piece (the treatment of refugees and asylum seekers). During this period, many interviews with the refugees themselves, on whose behalf the company feels it is speaking, also took place. Hence, although these people were not actually present in workshops and rehearsals, their impact and influence on the creative process, especially in its early phases, was essential to its development. The in-depth knowledge of the subject matter developed by the performers through their research process allowed them the authority to challenge aspects of the writing and direction which they felt were misguided or likely to mislead the audience. The early stages of this process then, were clearly collaborative. The stage of shaping and structuring returned to a more traditional format, but the performers' authoritative knowledge and personal experience of the material allowed them to contribute to the overall perspective taken on the material, making both their own voices heard and those of other, absent, collaborators, whom they felt they represented.

Freshwater describes theatre O's *Delirium*, co-produced with the Barbican and the Abbey Theatre, Dublin, as a 'step up', part of the company's aim to make the transition from small to medium-scale theatre. It is interesting that for devising-based companies this transition frequently involves creating an adaptation of an existing text. The most successful British devising companies (in terms of production at established theatres), Shared Experience, Kneehigh and Complicite, all develop the majority of their work from existing texts. Gecko, who made their own 'step up' subsequent to the project documented here, also chose to do an adaptation (of Gogol's *The Overcoat*) for the first time.[7] Does this indicate that mainstream venues, while they are attracted by devising as a genre, are not wholly willing to accept purely devised work? New companies and styles of work can bring in new audiences but theatres must balance this against the risk of alienating their loyal base audiences. Perhaps they see an adaptation as a safe bet in terms of the type of audiences they normally attract.

While it was a new departure for theatre O to work collaboratively with a playwright, the character-based, narrative form of their previous shows demonstrates their preference for story-based theatre. For Walsh, this would be the first time that he had worked creatively with a company rather than delivering a pre-written playscript. As with *Unstated*, Walsh sat in on rehearsals so there was creative feedback between him and the rest of the team and space was created for discussions between cast and writer and for off-text improvisation. The performers' creative contribution centred around character-building, which is an important element of the kind of Lecoq-influenced work theatre O produce. Much of the base work on Dostoevsky's text however had been done by Alford with Walsh before rehearsals began and Alford took the leading role in shaping the visual and physical aspects of the production. Again, time was an issue. The company benefited from the space and technical resources the Barbican could provide, but larger theatres are bound by commercial imperatives and are not set up to allow for the kinds of long, inclusive, experimental creative processes undertaken by, for instance, Third Angel. Alford particularly refers to wanting more time *between* phases of the creative process, to allow ideas to incubate.

In terms of authorship, then, although the presence of a writer within a devising process can limit the creative input of performers, focusing the collaboration more between writer and director, devising-based approaches do provide a model and a range of strategies which facilitate a responsive relationship between the playwright and the company not available within more traditional forms of writers' theatre. The simple presence of the writer in rehearsal opens up a dialogue which can offer different perspectives and opportunities to explore ideas physically, visually and interactively before the script is finalised.

The devising process

For the sake of clarity we will frame this discussion of the devising process in terms of the following stages: generation of initial ideas; exploration and development of ideas; shaping of material into a structured piece; performance and production; reflection. Although it was possible to identify these phases in most of the processes discussed in this book, they took very different forms since the kinds of external factors discussed above – levels of funding, time constraints, space, venue schedules, the involvement of commissioners – all impact upon how companies structure their creative process, as of course do their artistic aims. It is also important to note that the different stages are not always clearly defined, that they often overlap and that the devising process as a whole tends to be cyclical, as is exemplified in a consideration of how initial ideas emerge.

Initial ideas and starting points

The ideas behind each of the productions explored here had a lengthy genesis. Our writers usually choose the first day of rehearsal that they witness as the starting point of their studies, but there is always a 'backstory', often dating back years, during which ideas were incubating, people were meeting, a range of circumstances were coming together that made that first day possible.

Many devising companies have an area of interest to which they return repeatedly, producing a kind of 'family relationship' between their different shows. Very often shows arise directly out of previous projects. For example, Station House Opera's *The Other is You* was a further development of a multi-location structure already explored in two earlier productions and is related to the company's long-standing fascination with concepts of time, space and the contested nature of reality. Similarly, The Red Room's *Unstated* focused on material generated during the company's previous project, *Journeys to Work*.

The collaborative principle which underpins so much devising means that relationships themselves can provoke ideas: having worked together in a variety of contexts over a number of years, Gecko's Allel Nedjari and Amit Lahav wanted to undertake an in-depth exploration of their own close but conflicted relationship, while theatre O were keen to develop the relationship they had established with Enda Walsh during previous work at the National Theatre Studio. One might conclude that the *Shunt Lounge* arose out of a desire to re-examine company inter-relationships, in that it was designed to provide the individual artists with opportunities to rediscover and develop their individual artistic identities and thus reinvigorate their collaborative approach.

These examples demonstrate the cyclical nature of devising as a methodology, showing that, as so many of the practitioners included here insist, a devising process is never finished. Each production raises issues and questions which feed into the next. They also highlight the important fact that ideas can take time to mature or to find their place within a company's ongoing development of themes and concerns.

Devising practitioners often claim that they do not know, at the beginning, where they will get to at the end and, while this holds truer for some of the styles of work represented here than for others, all the projects included material that emerged during the creative process. Even when working from an existing story which prescribes essential elements of scenes and characters, as was the case with Faulty Optic and theatre O, the absence of a script in the early stages of the process leaves plenty of room for experimenting with *how* the story will be told. For other companies, notably Third Angel and Gecko, the sense of what they are aiming for changes markedly as the project progresses and this openness to discovery is a defining factor of their creative identities. In Jackie Smart's chapter, Amit Lahav of Gecko emphasises the importance of not 'closing down' the potential areas of creative exploration.

Exploration and development

It is perhaps within this stage that companies' stylistic and/or methodological heritage has the greatest influence, though it is interesting to note how many exploratory techniques cut across methodological boundaries. The companies considered here actively resist letting a style become a straitjacket. They like to move on, try new approaches, work with different people. A factor frequently reiterated by practitioners at our symposium and illustrated in a number of chapters is the willingness to use any method or technique which seems to work within the context of a given project. A degree of play was evident in all the devising processes described here. What we mean by 'play' is both the willingness to improvise around ideas and the degree of strategic flexibility purposefully left within the process, with many companies delaying fixing their pieces until a very late stage, a strategy common to companies within quite different stylistic traditions.

The political aims of The Red Room inform its long research process, and it is out of this process that characters and perspectives on the theme emerge. An important effect of the time dedicated to research is to ensure that all the creative participants in *Unstated* become immersed in the source material and develop a corresponding investment in it. We can see the influence of a different kind of political performance here: participatory or community theatre. Although *Unstated* is not a participatory piece, it is very much about the community of refugees and their concerns. As a campaigning company, The Red Room also aims to affect the audience's attitudes to the political status and human experience of refugees, and this provokes its experiments with space, leading it away from a straightforward end-on performance towards a more immersive experience.

The notion of transforming the space of reception as well as performance is rooted in performance art and live art traditions so one expects this concept to play an important role in the processes of companies such as Station House Opera and Shunt, for whom site-responsive performance is a modus operandi. In Station House Opera's *The Other is You*, the performance space is pre-defined by the structure of the triptych screens and 'rules' are set by the technical constraints. Improvisation takes place within these limitations, creating a tightly focused period of exploration of a defined set of themes. In contrast, the Shunt artists contributing to the *Lounge* have almost unlimited freedom to play within the particular space each of them chooses. Third Angel and the People Show also play with transforming space as a developmental activity. Like Shunt, these companies bring to the rehearsal room a wide range of objects and materials, not necessarily directly connected to the themes they aim to explore; making and using things in tangible ways forms an essential source of inspiration and exploration.

Playing with objects and materials is a technique which is not limited to companies with roots in art-based or postmodern traditions. The two physical theatre companies featured employ it too. Freshwater gives an example of how a problem with exposition in developing theatre O's *Delirium* was addressed through the use of scrap paper, and Gecko's improvisations were often inspired by things they happened to find lying around in their various rehearsal spaces.

This brings us to an idea that has become almost a cliché of devising: that some of the best ideas arise by accident or out of 'left field'.

As we see in the chapters on Faulty Optic, the People Show and Shunt, devising processes will often be deliberately structured in order to include chance and serendipity. The apparently spontaneous inspirations that such strategies provoke often emerge from the creators' heightened sense of awareness and a general openness to environment and to the devising group. A connected conceptual area is that of the performer's 'instinct' or intuition. Heddon and Milling raise this issue, citing the frequency with which performers say that they 'just knew' when something worked or that it 'felt right' (p. 10). 'Intuition functions paradoxically within improvisation in the devising process,' they argue: 'that moment of intuitive recognition in a group, as a group, is a function of the establishment of a shared set of patterns and experience' (ibid). When examined in depth such instances are often shown to be a product of a performer's underlying train of thought or search for a solution to a given problem. In his chapter on Faulty Optic's *Dead Wedding*, Moss gives a fascinating illustration of this when he describes how the company hit upon the image which would represent the character of Eurydice.

Stages of process: shaping material

Before we examine specific techniques and strategies used to edit, shape and structure ideas into a performance, it is important to emphasise that the two phases of generating material and organising it are often indistinct and simultaneous rather than consecutive. For this reason it might be more accurate to conceive of them as modes of thinking that might be in simultaneous operation. Guy Claxton writes in *Navigating the Unknown*: 'the conscious process of selecting and assessing ideas weaves in and out of their generation, as if there were a separate part of the mind, active at the same time as the generative part, monitoring and commenting on the creative process as it goes along' (2006, p. 65).

The structural principles that each company applies depend to a large extent on the style of work it is involved in. For theatre O, there are issues of translation from page to stage and, perhaps inevitably, the 'authority' of the source text becomes a matter for debate as the company aims to make the story its own. For the more visually oriented companies, structural principles are more compositional than narrative, even where a story is being told. Faulty Optic, for instance, emphasises mood and seeks recurring motifs in *Dead Wedding*. The People Show's structural process on *#118 The Birthday Tour* is revealing of a struggle between their usual traditions of looking for links through images, objects and actions and the more character-based and narrative terms which this production seems to create.

Because it involves communication about the meaning of a show and how to get that meaning across to an audience, the work of structuring a production brings into sharp focus the question of collaborative methodology. We have already discussed issues related to this; what we are interested in here is how the different formations play out in terms of specific strategies that companies use for shaping their work. One noteworthy realisation is how many innovative techniques companies have for articulating and discussing ideas: Shunt maintains a blog which provides a continuous forum for discussion and the exchange of ideas; company members of the People Show who have been working separately on scenes come together and take turns to 'narrate' the show to each other, so that all the participants have an opportunity to express their personal sense of how things fit together and what overall meaning or structure is emerging; as the joint artistic directors of Gecko create different ideas, they give them titles which they write on cards, shifting them around as their sense of the potential links between scenes develop, a technique also employed by theatre O. All these strategies enable company members to share responsibility for shaping the overall direction a production will take, although it should be noted that in most cases, even where there is not a single named director, someone will 'step out' in the later stages of the process to take on that role.

Another way of gaining an 'outside eye' is through work-in-progress presentations, whether these are internal to the company, for an invited audience of trusted friends or public performances. As a small-scale touring company, Gecko undertook a series of public work-in-progress performances at various regional venues. As Smart explains, this practice operates as an audience-development activity, designed to interest local people in both the company and the venue. Third Angel performed in a similar way at Chelsea Theatre for an audience largely made up of college and university drama students. This kind of work-in-progress is generally followed by a question-and-answer session with the audience. Third Angel's experimental methodology also led them to create a range of less conventional public events, including a balloon launch and a dinner party, which contributed to the development of *9 Billion Miles from Home* but were also stand-alone performances. The *Shunt Lounge* could be described as an ongoing work-in-progress performance, with the Shunt artists showing work at various stages of its development to friends, fans and whichever members of the public happen to come to the Vaults on a given night. Mermikides explains that some of the ideas

Shunt artists develop through the *Lounge* might be adopted or adapted for the large-scale shows.

Although it might seem risky to perform unfinished work publicly, in fact the way many work-in-progress performances are set up, including the fact that they are usually low-cost or free, tends to produce a sympathetic audience who are appreciative of the opportunity to engage with the creative process. In fact, *Guardian* theatre reviewer Lyn Gardner writes that the growth in work-in-progress performances suggests 'that there's a growing audience out there ... that is becoming increasingly fascinated more with process than product' (Gardner, 2008). For the performers, such work-in-progress performances provide a safe space to experiment and try out ideas. Whatever form they take, work-in-progress presentations prove to be significant factors in a production's development, often facilitating major steps forward or key changes in direction.

Stages of process: performance and reflection

The main thing that emerges about the performance stage is that it is not singular, and this cuts across methodological and stylistic differences between companies. Shunt, in particular, throws into doubt any assumptions that a creative process is a straightforward journey from intention to realisation; the *Lounge* is a continuous churning of variously 'finished' performances. Practitioners repeatedly claim that a devised work is never finished and this proved to be very much the case with the productions observed for this book. Evolution and development continue through the run of performances with quite substantial changes sometimes being made, as in Gecko's *The Arab and The Jew*.

This ongoing development brings with it an accompanying sense of ongoing reflection; if you never consider a production 'over', there is never a reason to stop thinking about how it might be developed or improved. Reflection is, in fact, an essential element of every stage of process: all the companies we feature constantly discuss creative decisions about the project in hand. Moreover, the notion of reflection includes an ongoing consideration of each company's – and indeed each artist's – techniques, strategies and approaches to process; as we pointed out earlier, most devising practitioners wish to avoid the straitjacket of a given style or methodology in order to retain the flexibility to respond appropriately to a range of creative projects. This commitment to reflection is what motivated these artists to participate in the research process which has led to this book. We hope that you will enjoy as much inspiration as we have in sampling the vibrancy of current devising practice.

If so, then this book will have achieved its aim, to provide aspiring devisers with a range of examples that they can draw on, in a way that allows them to contextualise their own work. Part of this contextualisation might be about the very definition of their work as devising: if devising is not defined by its distinction from script-led theatre or by its commitment to democratic and inclusive collaboration, what then characterises it today? The chapters in this book might suggest a tentative definition centring on a certain playful openness: to a range of stimuli; to creative risk and experimentation; to the views and input of a variety of participants, including performers; to change and development throughout the process even beyond the first performance.

As we have previously stated, we do not intend the accounts of process here to be taken as recipes for how to devise. This is not because some sort of easy-to-follow instruction manual would not meet a demand. Our students, we suspect, sometimes lose patience with our insistence that there is no one way to devise, that every devising process is different and that we cannot tell them how to do it. Any 'how to' guide, though, would detract from what makes devising so popular to begin with: its adaptability to different contexts and group compositions, and its potential for constant innovation in terms of process as well as product.

One of the major conclusions we have drawn from the observation and analysis contained within this text is that method and technique arise out of and serve intention. While students may find specific exercises and strategies revealing or inspiring, it is very clear that context is everything in terms of the processes documented here. Gillian Lees of Third Angel summed up the book's purpose at our symposium when she described what she hoped to gain from participation in the project:

> [something] I like about devising work is that if you have an idea there are so many different forms or things you can draw on ... so it might be dance or visual art or whatever, but if, for some reason, you can't find the right form to fit that idea, it's nice to be able to look at others to see if perhaps their form is something that might work for you, and to constantly change your own practice as well.

Notes

1. Devising in Process, a symposium at the Shunt Vaults, London, 16 January 2008. Keynote address, *Ten Notes Towards Writing About Devising* by Deirdre Heddon and Jane Milling.

2. The People Show, www.peopleshow.co.uk (accessed 14 June 2009).
3. theatre O, www.everythingispermitted.co.uk (accessed 30 June 2009).
4. Complicite, www.complicite.org/about/ (accessed 30 June 2009).
5. The People Show, www.peopleshow.co.uk (accessed 14 June 2009).
6. Louise Blackwell, Fuel, interview with Jackie Smart, 18 May 2009.
7. Opened at the Lyric Theatre, Hammersmith, April 2009.

1
People Show in Rehearsal
People Show #118 The Birthday Tour

Synne K. Behrndt

This chapter discusses aspects of the People Show's devising process as they undertook an adaptation of *People Show #117 The Birthday Show* for a national tour. The result was *People Show #118 The Birthday Tour*, a show which itself generated two different versions: the first toured in the spring of 2007 to venues in Alsager, Poole, Brighton, Liverpool, Windsor and Manchester. After further reworking, the performance toured to venues in Newcastle, Wolverhampton, Luton, Bristol and Halesworth, culminating in a run at the People Show Studios in London in late November 2007.

The Birthday Show was originally conceived as a celebration of the company's 40th birthday, and used the company's extensive history and the People Show Studios' site as starting points for the devising. Although this show was the template for the subsequent *Birthday Tour* the adaptation process, which involved adapting the show to other venues and bringing in new cast members, provided the company with an opportunity to rework and rethink the show as a whole. The challenge was in restructuring and re-contextualising existing material, a process that drew on the devisers' ability to develop existing material whilst maintaining an overview of an emerging dramaturgy. The evolution of the performance, from an event with loosely connected sections to a performance with a clear through line and audience journey, offers an example of the way in which a devised performance begins to find its shape and settles into a structure. Moreover, and this is particularly significant in relation to the company's non-autocratic devising ethos, the changes and move towards cohesion were also prompted by the new devisers that the company invited into the process.

The company's insistence on a non-autocratic process is central to their ethos and practice. A non-autocratic process implies that the process is not led by one person's vision; rather it is open to everybody's agendas, contribution and ideas. Moreover, decisions are taken collectively and on the basis of a shared understanding of the piece. This is not to say that there are no conflicts or disagreements or that everyone will agree with everything; rather it implies an insistence on a performer-led process and ownership. This performer-led process, in which no single director plans, delegates, structures the rehearsals, or makes the final decisions, calls for self-directed performers and creative theatre artists who take responsibility for all aspects of both the process and theatre event itself. This also applies to the conceptual and structural aspects of the performance; thus as Lynn Sobieski has commented, the People Show's devising approach calls upon the performers' ability to maintain 'creative spontaneity whilst constantly being aware of the evolving structure of the piece' (Sobieski, 1994, p. 93). This chapter looks at some of the challenges that the People Show devisers faced when reconfiguring existing stage material for performance as a touring promenade show, and pays particular attention to the implications of the company's artist-led working process. The chapter is based on six rehearsal observations between February and March 2007, a preview of the spring tour version and three performances of the autumn tour version.

For other discussions of the company's devising process see also Kirby (1974), Heddon and Milling (2006), Long (1971) and Peter Hulton's interview with Mark Long (1981).

The company's ethos and context

The People Show formed in 1966; with 119 original shows to date, the company is often cited as the UK's longest standing devising company (Heddon and Milling, 2006, p. 76). Indeed, as John Elsom affectionately remarks, the company deserves a special award for sheer survival (1995, p. 844). The company's role in introducing an alternative and experimental performance aesthetic to a British theatre audience cannot be overestimated and its influence is demonstrated in the extent to which devised theatre continues to be identified with aesthetic, structural and formal innovation.

The People Show formed after poet, painter and sculptor Jeff Nuttall invited Mark Long, John Darling and Sid Palmer to perform in a one-off happening in Powys Gardens, Notting Hill Gate. Undecided as to whether or not it was a success, they nevertheless decided to form a 'more solid relationship' (Long cited in Rees, 1992, p. 31), and together with Laura Gilbert they went on to perform their first Nuttall-scripted show, entitled *The People Show #1* (1966), in Better Books' basement on the Charing Cross Road. Hereafter the company's shows were given a number (*People Show #1, #2, #3* and so on) alongside specific titles. The first *People Show* set the agenda for the company's mixed media approach to performance, and it showed their penchant for process, the body, space, image and the anarchic and improvisational. Robert Hewison discusses *People Show #1*:

> Their first event in the Better Books basement was literally a people show, in that the performers stood as living sculptures, parts of their bodies exposed through cut-outs in screens, while they spoke their lines. The fine-art tradition of visual as opposed to verbal communication encouraged an exploration of process rather than product. ... Dada, collage and found objects contributed an element of chance, both the performers' bodies as kinetic sculptures, and the space in which they happened to be, called for responses that lay outside the control of any writer or director.
>
> (Hewison, 1986, p. 192–3)

The company then went on to perform a *People Show* every third week or so, and an invitation from renowned director Joan Littlewood to perform *People Show #9 Mother* (1967–8) at Stratford East helped to consolidate their growing reputation as an innovative and unorthodox company whose diverse practice ranged from events in night clubs to studio theatre shows. They subsequently received a host of invitations from festivals and venues, nationally as well as internationally, often choosing to create their shows on-site from found space, objects and even people.

The company retained a flexible structure in which artists could join specific projects, although founder members Nuttall and Palmer had left for good by 1968. Of the original members only Mark Long remains, with George Khan and Chahine Yavroyan from the company's early years still very much active in the company. Younger artists, such as Sadie Cook, Fiona Creese, Gareth Brierley, Jessica Worrall, and Nik and Rob Kennedy have since joined, making the People Show uniquely able to offer a space in which different generations devise side by side. This cross-generational balance is fundamental to their fertile practice and arguably one of the reasons why the company has sustained a prolific practice for more than 42 years. Moreover, new members' artistic practice will inevitably influence the company's work, direction and approach to devising, and the devisers' reference points in terms of what they perceive to be interesting contemporary practice naturally also can vary. This may also explain why the company, as well as their work, can be experienced as a hybrid melting pot of practices, cultures and approaches. In fact, one could say that radical inclusion, as opposed to exclusion, is central to the company's original ethos.

The company is currently based in London's Bethnal Green at the People Show Studios, an old church hall which they have converted into a facility where they have everything from workshops, an audiovisual suite, kitchen, residency and administrative office, studios and performance venue under the same roof. The building hosts the company's own rehearsals as well as visiting companies for whom the Studios are popular production facilities. Moreover, the company hosts what they call Building shows.

Despite their unique place in British theatre, the People Show's emphasis on democratic and non-autocratic processes is also testament to, and to some extent a product of, the company's cultural and artistic roots. The company emerged from the explosion of experimentation in the 1960s, a period defined on the one hand by a prevailing search for personal liberation, autonomy and authenticity (Hewison, 1986, p. xiii) and on the other hand by global political activism, radical reform and artistic and social experimentation. Artists and performance makers were changing the landscape of British theatre and re-examining how, why and for whom theatre was being produced, a process, which, as Rees comments, caused 'experimentation to happen on a broad front' (1992, p. 10). For more discussion of this period in UK theatre see also Davies (1987).

The British alternative theatre movement was a broad church and, as Kershaw observes, it encompassed quite an ideological range and political spectrum (Kershaw, 1992, p. 4). Hammond suggests that we might think of alternative theatre in terms of two main strands: on the one hand, theatre as an instrument of political change, or 'agit-prop', and on the other, avant-garde theatre with its 'radical exploration of our aesthetic perceptions and ideas about culture' (cited in DiCenzo, 1996, p. 18). Hammond places the People Show in the latter grouping, describing them as anarchic and iconoclastic. Yet, however different their aesthetic and thematic choices, companies such as Welfare State, CAST, Red Ladder and the People Show shared an interest in bringing new work to audiences who did not have 'social and geographical access to it' (Rees, 1992, p. 9) as well as embracing the freedom of making theatre 'without stage, rows of seats, lighting, sound equipment and director' (Long cited in Rees, 1992, p. 32).

If the British alternative theatre's experimentation was fuelled by a complex set of social, artistic and political motives, the People Show's work challenged audiences and critics to find new languages with which to describe it. Broadly categorised as 'performance art', their work might seem closer in spirit to the performance culture of the United States than of the UK, where it developed out of the cross-disciplinary and artistic experimentation of the late 1950s and 1960s American New Theatre. Within a British theatre culture that, according to Lynn Sobieski, has often had a 'strong literary bias' (1994, p. 89) and in which the emphasis on placing a play or text at the centre of interpretation has often generated a representational notion of plot, place, time and character development, the People Show's integration of techniques and compositional ideas from multiple art forms can make their work seem more consonant with the American new theatre's sculptural and painterly approach.

Within the company's work, linear representational structures are often abandoned in favour of a dramaturgy of event, an approach which Hans-Thies Lehmann describes as a structure in which acts are 'real in the here and now and find their fulfilment in the very moment they happen, without necessarily leaving any traces of meaning' (2006, p. 104). This does not mean that there is no meaning or narrative in their work. The People Show's theatre prompts a re-examination of the classical notions of plot and storytelling, prompting Sandy Craig to comment that critics have floundered when getting to grips with the company's performances, preferring to describe them as 'structured around a collage of atmospheres rather than narrative or character' (1980, p. 24). Not surprisingly, the company's work has invited impressionistic accolades such as 'visual, theatrical, imagistic', or 'Dadaist, irreverent, atmospheric and dreamlike' (Sobieski, 1994, p. 92).

Approach to process

The company's non-autocratic approach to process and performance is currently reflected in their organisational structure where, instead of an artistic director, a steering group consults with a wide network of People Show associate artists on future projects and planning. This fluid infrastructure makes the company more a collective than a permanent ensemble and, as their artistic policy states, the company and their work remain 'informed by the personalities and skills of the individuals working within the company at any given time'.[1] This point is reiterated by Victoria Nes Kirby when she observes that in order to understand their 'working techniques', one has to understand 'the people themselves as artists. Their work is truly what they are as people, and it is their respect for and reactions to each other's ideas that are responsible for the unique qualities of their shows' (Kirby, 1974, p. 49). The People Show deliberately encourages an open door policy where artists from different artistic, cultural and educational backgrounds collaborate on a project-to-project basis. Thus over the years more than a hundred different collaborators, artists and performers have contributed to the company, amongst them musician and film maker Mike Figgis, performance artist Roland Miller and Mexican painter José Nava, to name but a few.

This fluid and flexible approach is also reflected in the way in which company members naturally adopt roles and responsibilities within the process as befits their personalities or interests. While there is this scope for engaging individual skills and explorations, it is also assumed that the People Show deviser must take responsibility for all aspects of the process and the production. On a practical level, this means unloading the truck and building the set when on tour, and Mark Long admits that this way of working can be a shock to people who work with them for the first time: needless to say, it is not to everyone's liking.[2] However, this level of involvement with the production also reflects the company's artistic belief that ownership of the work is born from an intimate understanding of the process in all its details, including lights, sound, costume, set design, movement and so on, and that this enables the deviser to propose interesting solutions to a variety of challenges. This belief partly explains the company's insistence on the performer-led devising process.

The company maintains that there is no typical People Show devising process. In fact, Long has explained that every process begins with doubt as to whether they will have a show at the end because there is 'no definite method to fall back on' (in Hulton, 1981–2, p. 5); every process is different because the circumstances and the people are different. In general, though, they are less interested in devising from a specific theme, concept or idea, preferring to start from a 'visual point of view' (ibid, p. 8). This could be a spatial structure, set design, image, a painting or object(s). Other processes might start with the devisers' individual projects, current 'obsessions' or explorations. Whilst working out how to create the most flexible structures, or find a way into the material, or even just working out whether the material has any potential, the devisers are simultaneously on the look-out for 'something', a *clue* that might help focus the material and join together everyone's different interests. Long has explained:

Generally when you start a show, there'll be one big clue that will open it up. And it is finding that clue that takes the time. That big clue might be the set ... it might be a piece of equipment, it can be a very small thing, it might be a costume, it might be one character, but often you'll find that one idea suddenly moves over something that everybody sympathizes with.

(Long, in Hulton, 1981–2, p. 7)

If this sounds somewhat abstract, in real terms it has to do with working out *what* is holding together a potential structure. Once this elusive clue reveals itself and more tangible ideas start coming into focus, the devisers can begin to layer and enrich the material, and look for ways in which ideas can be expanded. Long has described a process whereby they generate a series of visual images and then 'embroider' the images with their bodies, words and reactions. This process of 'embroidering' might be understood as a way of layering and adding texture to an image: the more you begin to explore an image, the more detail you discover and add. Long describes it as a way of 'enlarging the images for the audience' (1971, p. 57). The devisers do not necessarily set out to tell a specific story; rather they might want to evoke a certain sensation or atmosphere through a structure, something which leaves it more open for the audience to piece together episodes or images into complex narratives.

Although the company's approach has developed over the years, Jeff Nuttall's original interest in composing with behaviour, objects and space, in which scripts are conceived as 'hooks on which to hang the disparate vocabulary, visual, obtuse, abstract, absurd, of the happening' (1979, p. 39), still seems present in the company's process. Rejecting dramatic theatre's representational structures, the scripts could be seen as task-based scores for structured improvisation with room for the performers' own ideas, contributions and interpretations. Thus any character, story or motivation will develop from tasks and actions as opposed to a defined content – an approach which is anchored in the company's early explorations. Long recalls Nuttall's instructions in which the performers were encouraged to be themselves, use their intuition and respond to the moment. For example, in *People Show #1* (1966), the script simply said 'Discuss situation with audience' (Long, 1971, p. 49). With no plot or character to hide behind the performers were encouraged to put the reality of their interpersonal relationships 'on stage', a situation which pushed them into unknown and often risky territory. As Long explains, the idea was to put 'two people in a situation where you know it can explode, and also putting yourself in a relationship to the audience where you know you can explode' (ibid). This level of transgression between what is real and what is staged, the slippage between 'persona' and performer, remains a recurring feature and dramaturgical device in their work. 'Character' is indeed a slippery notion in the People Show's work.

People Show #118 The Birthday Tour: adapting *The Birthday Show*

People Show #117 The Birthday Show (2006) was devised to celebrate the company's 40-year history and involved a number of past and present People Show collaborators. Created within the People Show Studios, the show was conceived as a promenade event in which the audience travelled between individual installations and performances. Sadie Cook has described the original show as 'a big explosion' intent on incorporating and bringing together decades of different People Show members' input and perspectives.[3] From this explosion of different and multiple perspectives, the company set out to explore a few central ideas and perhaps to create a more cohesive performance that could tour to different venues and play to audiences who were not necessarily familiar with the company's long history. It should be mentioned that *The Birthday Tour*'s devising process was in many ways an unusual one for the company, in that the devising was primarily focused on adapting an existing structure, meaning that their process was largely dictated by logistical and practical circumstances.

When working on *People Show #118 The Birthday Tour*, the process might be summed up as a task of problem-solving which meant that the devisers had to adapt and rethink moments, situations, images and scenarios. A simple example would be the way in which the reconfiguration of a dining table (and thereby a new spatial figuration) prompted a starting point for rethinking one of the sections in the show (Act 3). In *The Birthday Show*, a dining table was used as a thrust stage, with the audience seated around it, but in order to accommodate other venues and audience numbers the table had to be turned sideways, something which changed the stage–audience relationship to one suggesting the perspective of the proscenium arch. Cook comments:

> It changed our content because the simple move of turning the table from one way to another meant that we had to re-devise a lot of what happened. ... It then sparked off other things because the table in

> that position was very reminiscent of old classic art, ... the *Last Supper* being the obvious example, which is then referenced in this piece with the frozen moment in *Act 3* where we adopt certain poses.[4]

As Cook explains, the process was not about tweaking details; rather, practical circumstances such as the shifting of the table meant that they to rethink the performance on a more fundamental level. One can perhaps compare it with what might happen if, having built a house, the owner kept adding details and refinements until the building is altered to the point that it becomes a new house. One can still see fragments and traces of the old structure, thus creating an interesting palimpsest structure in which the original and the new merge and blend. For the devisers, the task is to observe and to recognise the emergence of a new structure, even whilst chipping away at the existing one.

The fact that the company generally creates all its material through improvisation and practical problem-solving *in situ* in rehearsal, as opposed to implementing predetermined decisions, means that this adaptation process calls on the performers' ability to 'cut and paste' and rethink existing material. One could perhaps liken this adaptation process to what Eugenio Barba has called the performer's 'montage'. Taking inspiration from Kabuki performers, Barba proposes that within an improvisation a performer can make use of material and situations that have been 'prepared for other scenic situations' and can draw upon this material when the opportunity arises, thus presenting the material in a new context (Barba and Savarese, 1991, p. 160). To put it differently, the performer has a set of 'presets' (for example gestures, images, situations, movement, text), and can call on these within an improvisation whilst being aware of how the changing context will impact on the material.

This notion of 'presets' may become clearer if we consider the way in which new performers such as Tyrone Huggins were eventually incorporated into the adapted Act 3. Huggins had created an installation for *The Birthday Show*, but for *The Birthday Tour* version the company decided to leave out the installation, and bring Huggins into the new Act 3. They were interested in retaining some of the original installation's themes, images and ideas, and at various times during their improvisations they would refer to something from the installation that they thought could be recycled in the new performance. It is important to understand that a 'preset' may not always be something very concrete, such as a gesture or an object, but it can be a particular feeling, or spatial dynamic. At one point the installation is referred to in terms of how it made an audience member feel. It can be difficult to translate a feeling concretely but the devisers can be aware of a particular kind of atmosphere which they want to explore or evoke. Thus 'atmosphere' or a particular experience of space could also be a form of 'preset'. Moreover, the company's own history and their catalogue of 117 past performances might also be seen as a form of 'preset', as was the case with both *The Birthday Show* and *Tour* performances, because they took the company's own history as a starting point. For example, the devisers, especially when stuck, will remind each other of images, objects, actions and ideas from previous shows. Thus all these things taken together become a box of material that the devisers can 'plunder' and graft into their new improvisations.

A recurring strategy in the People Show's process is to start from tableau, image or gesture and then develop a sequence of actions until they are able to identify an outline or rough sketch. Initially the devisers focus on finding the shape and contours of a scene and will then work on filling in details and adding colour. They focus on the 'how' and solving concrete problems such as finding transition and how to get from one moment, or image, to another. The devisers explore the many ways in which the journey might be made, and suggestions are often prefaced with 'wouldn't it be fun if ...?'

Let us consider a moment in detail. When working on Act 3, Fiona Creese, Gareth Brierley, Tyrone Huggins and Mark Long are adapting a series of images and loosely developed scenarios from *The Birthday Show*: Brierley's monologue about birthday presents; Creese appearing on cue from a box with a gun; a balloon; a choreographed fight scene between Brierley, Huggins and Creese (with over-sized boxing gloves on her feet) and a fencing scene between Huggins and Brierley. These are shaped into a structure through a process of probing the moment: 'What could come next?'; 'What might then happen?; 'How and when does Creese appear?'; 'How does she end up on the chair?'; 'How do Brierley and Huggins make contact?'; 'How does the fight begin?'; 'What does she do with the gun?' and 'How does Huggins end up with the gun?'. They offer solutions by trying out concrete ideas and gradually start to discover dynamics and even dramatic suspense.

As mentioned earlier Tyrone Huggins was not in *The Birthday Show's* Act 3, and whilst they explore his journey from moment to moment they are simultaneously wrestling with questions about *who* and *what* he may be within the context of the new Act 3. The introduction of Huggins in Act 3 calls for an exploration of a new story, or narrative thread. For example, at the beginning of the fight scene between Brierley and Huggins, Brierley pulls out different kinds of 'weapons' from a cardboard box; Creese suggests to Huggins that his 'weapon' has to be a sinister object, like a human bone, because Huggins seems to carry a mystery – could it be the bone of a dead woman? Creese contemplates that there might be another story embedded in Act 3 which they have yet to discover; she remembers a discussion earlier in the rehearsal where they suggested that Huggins could be a kind of magician, a master of ceremonies with a dark secret. In trying to work out what the object could be, they are simultaneously devising and finding out more information about Huggins's 'character'. Does he carry a secret?

This is also typical of the way the company will try to discover the overall thrust of the scene and the interpersonal relationships of the 'characters' within it, not through psychological reasoning but by getting a *feel for* the atmosphere, tempo and dynamic of a scene. They are not heard discussing psychological intention or motivation; instead they often explore something through action, rhythm and image, often looking for ways in which to create dramatic tension, or 'a strong moment'. An improvisation might unfold, only for one of the devisers to say, 'this doesn't seem right' or 'that feels right'. This may then prompt someone to step out, have a look at the scene, take stock and make observations on how it looks or communicates from an audience's point of view. Once a basic outline has been agreed, the devisers start a layering process, adding details and other actions.

In rehearsal, they often look for ways in which they can complicate, enrich and layer a moment or scene, thus making their exploration alternate between, on the one hand, playing with random associations, ready-made actions and images from *The Birthday Show* and, on the other, pragmatic problem-solving. If we imagine that the outline of a scene moves from A to B, the journey between the two points is repeatedly delayed, expanded or deferred, as more actions or moments are added and interspersed. For example, during a mock fight scene, Sadie Cook and Fiona Creese propose that they might 'pause' or interrupt the fight with a comedy moment in which Cook pretends to 'bang' Creese's head against a wall. This interruption produces an erratic rhythm and dynamic, which sets off a chain of associations and prompts them to explore other actions or moments.

Sound and rhythm play an important role in this layering. The often-used juxtaposition of erratic and offbeat sounds creates the sense of a chaotic event, a cacophony of action, live music and sound effects building to a crescendo and climax. Yet despite this appearance of chaos, the scene is meticulously choreographed. The devisers are alert to the possibility that a scene or moment might need more, or less, pace, volume, chaos, stronger transition, contrast or counter point; sometimes a moment continues to be unresolved. When they get stuck, they keep the momentum by saying 'we've marked a problem', leave it and return to it when they 'know more' or 'have more information'. They trust that answers and solutions will reveal themselves once they have a clearer idea of the overarching shape of the piece, sometimes choosing to 'deposit' material or a specific idea in the 'memory bank', with the knowledge that they can make the 'withdrawal' when the opportunity presents itself. Sometimes being stuck leads to stock-taking where they rethink their strategy and perspective.

At one point during this process, the devisers come up against the classic devising conundrum of producing good material but not knowing quite what they are aiming for. Brierley steps out of the improvisation to get a clearer picture. He suggests that it might help if they think of the scene as a 'party game' – a dramaturgical intervention which suddenly gives the material a different direction. Brierley's intervention implicitly addresses the question surrounding why they, the 'characters', are doing what they are doing, and so the 'party game' provides a hook or a framing of the moment for the devisers. Here, the deviser shuttles between improvising and directing, sometimes looking at the material from outside, sometimes joining the improvisation and working out an idea from 'inside', then stepping out again to direct the scene.

This alternating movement where the devisers move in and out of a scene also prompts them to discover details that may be overlooked from inside the improvisation. Where an outside director, or dramaturg, will often notice significant details, the self-directed devisers need to find other strategies with which to embroider and add details. Sadie Cook recounts a situation when Brierley stepped out to look at a scene only to discover that within the scene Cook gives him a certain look. Because Brierley always had his back to her in the scene, he was unable to see it. Watching the scene from the outside he was able to spot it, step back into the scene and incorporate a reaction to Cook's gesture. This movement 'in' and 'out' challenges the self-directed devisers to develop a kind of double vision where, as Brierley describes, the performer develops a technique whereby s/he is inside a moment, present and performing it for real whilst at the same time being alert to the show as a whole and its structural possibilities and problems. Thus the devisers will develop their material with an acute dramaturgical awareness of how their actions impact on the whole performance event. Brierley goes on to explain that this process whereby the deviser engages with the show on an emotional, conceptual and structural level does not necessarily stop once the show is on tour. Each performance presents an opportunity to develop and discover new things.[5]

With no director keeping a record of changes and decisions, the performers also have to develop their own ways of retaining an overview. Some keep a notebook, occasionally dropping out of improvisations to make a note of something. During an improvisation for Act 3, Nicola Blackwell would consult her notebook and presented the others with an impressive list and analysis of different narrative threads that had emerged in the material so far, an observation which seemed vital for the company to gather together some of the many emerging sprawling threads. Another strategy is to narrate to one another, step by step, what happens in a scene. As they talk through the scene, plotting and detailing actions and transitions, they ask each other questions concerning 'what', 'why' and 'how'. By narrating and 'plotting' they are establishing everyone's journey in a scene, as well as imagining what the audience might see or experience. This attention to detail in their 'narration' technique enables them to understand and discuss a scene or the show's emerging inner logic and to flag up unresolved or unclear moments and transitions. A guiding principle is to ask what it means for them, as performers, to understand how they are making the journey from one thing to another, but at the same time try to imagine the action from the audience's perspective.

Another approach to taking stock of the material would be their formalised weekly work-in-progress sessions. These sessions, in which every one in the company – devisers, producer, sound designer, set designer, general manager and invited associate artists – share, view and then feed back on the material, once again demonstrate the company's ethos, the sense that the devising is a responsibility shared between everybody involved in the production. Moreover, the sessions are essentially the company's mechanism for ascertaining the direction of the work as well as discussing how the work can be developed, and how individual sections and moments relate to one another. It is clear that the company members respect each other as individual artists, in that they do not try to make anyone change their material; rather they try to figure out how it may add a new texture to the piece. One could perhaps describe it as a process whereby they initially do not ask each other to generate a particular kind of material, but rather try to work out how individual artists' contributions can sit within a piece. The shared sessions are therefore about encouraging each other's exploration whilst discussing the ramifications for the piece as a whole.

These shared sessions were particular necessary and useful when devising *The Birthday Tour* because the devisers were devising different sections in different spaces simultaneously. Whilst some were working on one section, others would be working on another. The 'cross-referencing' of material which the shared work-in-progress session provided also facilitated a greater understanding of the emerging structure in the performance, which led to discussions about whether or not they should make a concerted effort to join together the different sections and create a narrative thread. Or was *The Birthday Tour* perhaps more akin to an event in which the audience would promenade between self-contained happenings that connected loosely by way of shared themes? This discussion may become more concrete if we look at the example of the 'Black/White Room'. This section changed dramatically from the first to final version, prompted by changes in cast.

Devising on simultaneous tracks

As suggested earlier, the adaptation process was largely informed by practical problem-solving. In order to retain the original show's promenade aspect, the performance had to be condensed into four different sections which were performed in three different locations; the audience would travel to the main auditorium for the Prologue and Act 3 sections, to a coach parked outside for the Tour Bus section, and to an adjacent room for the Black/White Room section. In adapting the show for touring, the company were essentially emulating the promenade format by devising different sections of the show in separate spaces. Thus they would discover the parallels, or disjunctions, between the sections as they went along whils t reflecting on how these convergences would impact on the overall structure and content of the show. When Nicola Blackwell and Sadie Cook started re-devising the Black/White Room section for *The Birthday Tour* they were at the same time re-devising Act 3, a section which involved the whole ensemble. They were essentially alternating between devising one section from scratch whilst participating in the re-devising of the other section. Neither of them was in the original version of the Black/White Room and they decided to keep the original set design and costumes.

Cook comments that at first it was difficult to know what to do with the Black/White Room because none of the sections was 'fully formed'.[6]

Instead of trying to force or second-guess connections to the show's other sections, they took *The Birthday Show* themes 'past' and 'memory' as their starting points, and from there ended up with perhaps more tangential ideas such as technology, science, principles of randomness, time and perception. When they presented their first work-in-progress to the rest of the company, it was striking how different the material was from the other sections within the show. Where the Prologue, the Tour Bus and Act 3, as the show was progressing, could be said to connect through the thematic thread of 'theatre', 'People Show' and 'memory', and certainly the Tour Bus could be experienced as a back story to Act 3, the Black/White Room's atmosphere, texture, aesthetic and thematic thread evoked a very different piece. The company's producer Jane Corry commented that it felt like a contemporary dance piece. The company's first impulse was not to try to change the section, but rather to find a way of letting it be what it was.

The work-in-progress showing prompted a discussion about ways in which the form and content of the Black/White Room could impact on Act 3; could the Black/White Room's dreamy, ethereal and weight-less quality help evoke and suggest a sense of 'parallel universe', and if so might this somehow underpin the whole performance? Mark Long suggested that there was a sense that the Black/White Room was encroaching on Act 3, as if the Room's sprawling images and stories were spilling over into other sections of the show. Following on from Long's observations, Blackwell suggested that she could enter Act 3 and exit Black/White Room with the same gesture or movement, as if to suggest that she was travelling from one world to another, or that she was a performer who would suddenly find herself in a different show. The company discussion triggered further ideas about the ways in which the two sections could connect. It was suggested that it might be possible to mirror or replicate specific gestures, actions and objects; for instance, a costume, balloon and a radio from Black/White Room could appear in Act 3, thus creating a sense of a continuum in which objects and stories would *travel* across the rooms. This could also apply to sound or the repeated use of a music motif; for example sound designer Nik Kennedy suggested that the sound of the radio could appear in both sections. Alternatively, one could be subtle and have the radio object appear in one section and the sound of a radio in another. This would prompt the audience to link or connect the two sections on a more subliminal level.

The devisers are then on the lookout for ways to join up the different sections. During an improvisation in rehearsals for Act 3, Blackwell would suggest that the glitter ball could link Act 3 to the Black/White Room section; for instance, she could enter Act 3 carrying the glitter ball, which the audience would recognise from the Black/White Room. It is characteristic of the way in which the company discusses the material that the devisers do not want to be too heavy handed or too explicit in their signposting, rather they always look to create a structure and logic whereby the audience can fill in the gaps themselves.

The final show

The Birthday Tour finally seemed to fall into place, achieve more cohesion and 'feel more balanced' as Gareth Brierley put it, once the company had resolved the Black/White Room.[7] Thus the reworking of the Black/White Room also became a catalyst for creating a greater sense of cohesiveness for *The Birthday Tour* as a whole. The Black/White Room section had undergone the most radical changes throughout the process, and Cook describes the first reworking for *The Birthday Tour* as a stand-alone piece.[8] Although the section's exploration of science, time, principles of randomness, memory and perception were nominally related to *The Birthday Tour's* overarching thematic focus, the link was perhaps too tangential to be realised fully. Thus the Black/White Room's very exciting, but also radically different, first reworking made this section sit apart from the rest of the material in the show. In one way one could argue that an inclusion of difference is part and parcel of the People Show experience, and that the audience are encouraged to take delight in this difference. However, as Gareth Brierley comments, after the first version of *The Birthday Tour* some audience, and company, feedback suggested that the performance's fragmented nature could be overly disparate and confusing and seemed in need of clearer structure and editing.[9] Sadie Cook comments that, especially in their preparation for the autumn tour, the company's overarching discussions revolved around imagining and understanding the audience's journey through the show.[10]

Thus the development of the Black/White Room continued as the autumn version of *The Birthday Tour* underwent yet another re-working, and due to other commitments Bernadette Russell had to take over from Nicola Blackwell. Russell had seen the two previous versions as an audience member, and thus the re-devising process of the Black/White Room started with Russell relaying to Sadie Cook what she, as an audience member, had observed about the performance. Cook comments that Russell's objectivity and questioning became an important catalyst for thinking about the section's role within the overall structure. Russell observed that the Black/White Room was interesting on its own but her sense was that it needed stronger integration, and it needed to *serve* the show as a whole. She comments:

> I think in the original version with three other rooms there was enough breadth to support a space that didn't really connect with the others, but when that was downsized to two other spaces, it didn't make sense. It was important to me that it connected conceptually in a narrative way, in the broadest sense of that, to the rest of the show. [11]

The result of their reworking was a radical transformation of the Black/White Room in which, perhaps unusually for the company, the section had a dramatic story with a clear, if also fragmented, narrative in which characters, events and actions from the other sections were woven into its plot structure. Thus it literally set the scene for the final Act 3 in that it became a back story to the events and characters that we were to meet later on in the performance. It also made references, some explicit, some subtle, to events in the Prologue, Tour Bus and Act 3 sections, and these references gave the impression that the different stories, events and characters were all interconnected in one way or another. Moreover, the decision to devise the Black/White Room as a fragmented film noir detective story contributed to the overriding sense of mystery, strangers and secrets that permeated *The Birthday Tour* as a whole. The choice to frame the Black/White Room as a riddle or mystery in which even the 'characters' within it seemed confused about what was going on also gave the performance a licence to play fast and loose with the facts, so to speak. This linked well with the premise set in the Prologue, in which Mark Long's story about the company's history suggested that People Show were a company in which anything could, and probably would, happen.

Thus the Black/White Room had gone from being a self-contained, if conceptually very exciting, section to being the mechanism which pulled together the many different threads within the performance. It is interesting that the company's choice to have one section assist, join together, complement and give intention to the other sections made the performance more, not less, open to interpretation. This may have something to do with the delight audience members can take in intricate and subtle puzzles, riddles and mysteries – and the more complicated they seem the more they may want to pursue them. Even if there is no end point or resolution, the pursuit itself can be worth the effort.

The final version of *The Birthday Show* managed to produce a sense of mystery and secrecy particularly well.

By the time of *The Birthday Tour's* final performance, it had changed from being an event consisting of isolated scenarios and installations to becoming a more cohesive performance with a clearer journey for the audience. Although the company's approach to devising was to a large extent still informed by composing with atmosphere, sound, image and movement, as opposed to telling a particular story or representing dramatic characters, *The Birthday Tour* became a dramatic world in which the audience were invited to follow different narrative threads or even imagine 'characters'. Held together by a number of different threads and 'character' journeys, the narrative thrust of the piece could be seen as the alternation between two narrative levels: on one hand, the history of the theatre company, the People Show, a premise which was introduced in the Prologue; and on the other hand, a surreal party populated by eccentric and theatrical guests with hidden agendas, secrets and a shared past. Act 3 thus gathered the ensemble for one final performance. The fact that it became deliberately difficult to separate the two levels would suggest the obvious interpretation that the People Show *is* like a surreal party. The weaving together of these two main narrative threads produced a multi-layered composition inhabited by different self-contained stories. For example, although the Black/White Room carefully framed Act 3 through the theme of a party, it was also a self-contained detective story, or a story about mistaken identity.

There may be no such thing as a typical People Show process since circumstances, and importantly, the people involved will vary. The adaptation process that led to *The Birthday Tour* involved a set of complex logistical challenges which framed and informed the entire process. Thus in this case the company's approach to devising was greatly informed by the show's multi-spatial set-up, which perhaps made the process even more complex for the ensemble. The devising for *The Birthday Show* literally took place in all rooms of the People Show Studios at all times, with most of the company involved in devising more than one section, a devising scenario which stretched the devisers' need to retain an overview of the whole piece. This, combined with the fact that there is no single person that leads the work or retains the overview, can make the process seem very fluid, polyphonic and disorientating. But still, the exhausting and complicated nature of the process may also be what produces such an interesting tension between disciplined and loose structures, the real and the fictional, the controlled and the anarchic.

The People Show #118 The Birthday Tour (2007)

Company: Amelia Pimlott, Ben Carrick, Bernadette Russell, Chahine Yavroyan, Denis Buckley, Esther Renehan, Fiona Creese, Gareth Brierley, George Khan, Helen Stone, Jessica Worrall, Katie Kelly, Mark Long, Nick Tigg, Nik Kennedy, Nicola Blackwell, Richard Rudnicki, Rob Kennedy, Sadie Cook, Tyrone Huggins.
Producer: Jane Corry.
General Manager: David Duchin.

Chronology of selected productions

People Show #1, Better Books, Charing Cross Road, London, 1966.

People Show #9 Mother, Better Books, Charing Cross Road, London, 1967/68. Also performed at Stratford East.

People Show #24 Walter, Little Theatre, Sheffield, as part of the Sheffield Arts Festival. Also toured to Edinburgh, Glasgow and London.

People Show #64 The Boxer Show, 1976. Performed in Newcastle, Colchester, Belgium and Holland. It was performed in Amsterdam as *People Show #63* as part of the 10th anniversary celebration programme for Stichting Mickery Workshop, Amsterdam, Holland.

People Show #113 Film Club/Baby Jane, directed by Jessica Worrall, Traverse Theatre, Edinburgh, August 2003. Later opened at the Riverside Studios, London, January 2004.

People Show #115 Play Dead, People Show Studios, London, 19 May 2004. Opened at The Pod, Edinburgh, 4–29 August 2004. National Tour: Edinburgh Festival; Glasgow Arches; Bristol Young Vic; Bath Rondo; Theatre Royal Plymouth; Whitstable; Luton Hat Factory; Oxford Pegasus Theatre.

People Show #114 The Obituary Show, The Bush Theatre, London, 29 June– 23 July 2005. UK tour autumn 2005: Exeter Phoenix; New Theatre Royal, Portsmouth; Unity Theatre, Liverpool; Traverse Theatre, Edinburgh; Tobacco Factory, Bristol; Drum Theatre, Plymouth; Lighthouse, Poole; Riverside Studios, London.

The People Show #117 The Birthday Show, People Show Studios, London, 12–15 July 2006.

The People Show #118 The Birthday Tour, Alsager Arts Centre, 5 March 2007. Spring tour 2007: Lighthouse, Poole; Gardner Arts Centre, Brighton; Unity Theatre, Liverpool; Windsor Arts Centre, Windsor; Contact Theatre, Manchester.

Autumn tour 2007: Northern Stage, Newcastle; Arena Theatre, Wolverhampton; The Hat Factory, Luton; Tobacco Factory Theatre, Bristol; The Cut, Halesworth; People Show Studios, London.

The People Show #119 Ghost Sonata, directed by Josette Bushell-Mingo, Sefton Park Palm House, Liverpool, 22–27 April 2008.

Notes

1. The People Show, www.peopleshow.co.uk (accessed 30 September 2008).
2. Mark Long, conversation with the author, 16 November 2007.

3. Sadie Cook, interview with the author, 16 November 2007.
4. Ibid.
5. Gareth Brierley, interview with the author, 16 November 2007.
6. Cook, op cit.
7. Brierley, op cit.
8. Cook, op cit.
9. Brierley, op cit.
10. Sadie Cook, telephone conversation with the author, 4 March 2008.
11. Bernadette Russell, interview with the author, 16 November 2007.

2

Three-way Inter-play

Devising Processes and Critical Issues in Station House Opera's Telematic Performance, *The Other Is You*

Jem Kelly

Definition of technical terms

Immediacy: This refers to the reception and perception of the physical (phenomenal) body in performance, which tends to be immediate in theatrical performance: if a performer moves or speaks, the audience usually is aware of this instantaneously. In multimedia performances, such as *The Other Is You*, sometimes there is a time delay in the reception of video and audio elements. This works against immediacy and synchronicity of reception and perception of all the signifying elements perceived in relation to performed action.

Intermediality: This term has become synonymous with the interaction of different media in performance, primarily denoting intersections of video, sound and the performing body.

Ludic: Of games performed by rules; in *The Other Is You* mediated by the limits of camera angles and visual perspectives (c.f. Bourriaud's ideas about 'artistic activity' being 'a game', discussed later in this chapter).

Materiality: The performer's body functions both as a sign, or representation, and simultaneously as the material through which such signification takes place. In *The Other Is You* (as in many performances using video projection), there is a disparity or tension in the perception of the physical bodies of the performers and their two-dimensional representations on screens. This disparity draws attention to the actual (phenomenal) body of the performer and to the aesthetic role he or she performs, which is contrasted with the immateriality of the screened images.

Multiplicity: This refers to the many and varied systems of communication in intermedial performance, but also in the case of *The Other Is You* to the multiple representations of the performers, in the flesh and on screens.

Non-matrixed performance: This is a term coined by Michael Kirby (1995, p. 41) to describe performers whose presence and actions are not 'embedded ... in matrices of pretended or represented character, situation, place and time'.

Performance register: This refers to the relationship between the performer and the role he or she adopts. For example, in a naturalistic performance the performer may adopt the register of identification, whereas in Brechtian performance the register may be one of demonstration. In postdramatic performances, the performer may attempt to avoid adopting a register altogether, in which case the performance is 'non-matrixed'.

Post-linear temporality: In theatre, there is usually a temporal immediacy of action and its reception: what we see and hear usually occurs at the same time as it is perceived, unlike in cinema, for example, which depends on the earlier recording of images and sounds. In performances that rely on intermediality, there can be elements of the performance that do not occur simultaneously. This is the case with *The Other Is You*, in which elements of the performed action appear on screens later than the same action is perceived to be taking place in the physical performance spaces. As the video images depict action that took place some time later than they were performed, there is a constant call on the spectator's memory of action that has taken place.

Proxemics: This is the term used to denote the spatial layout of the performance location, and to the distances between the elements of performance (performers, screens, objects, cameras and audience).

Site-specificity: Some performances are devised exclusively around the physical dimensions of the spaces in which they are staged, as is the case with *The Other Is You*.

Telematics: The science of the long-distance transmission of computerised information, including video streaming.

Nine people from across the continent perform together in one single production. Three audiences in different cities experience the performance simultaneously. A basement in Brighton, a school in Groningen and a café in Berlin merge to become a fourth imaginary space.[1]

There is a reverent silence in the Brighton Basement prior to the scheduled performance of *The Other Is You* as spectators watch a triptych of live video images transmitted from Germany, Brighton and Holland and projected onto a wall behind the motionless performers. A camera in each space focuses on the physically present audience, and gradually people in each location identify their virtual selves onscreen and peer curiously at projected images of the distant spectators. Suddenly, a woman on the screen representing Germany lifts her arm; a little later a spectator in Holland responds, then, despite the two-second time-lag caused by Internet delay, the audiences in each of the spaces manage to co-ordinate their arms to produce a Mexican wave, creating a sequential movement simultaneously in three countries. This pan-European interaction of actual people with virtual representations is fundamental to *The Other Is You*, and the ludic reaction of physical bodies to projected images is a key feature carefully explored in the devising process.

The Other Is You produces a virtual community of remotely located performers and audiences that co-exist in a shared virtual space. The performance, a hybrid of physical actions (mostly task-based) and virtual representations, uses geographically located performers whose images are transmitted into cyberspace, where their actions appear to correlate. In his book *Relational Aesthetics,* Nicolas Bourriaud observes that 'Artistic activity is a game, whose forms, patterns and functions develop and evolve according to periods and social contexts' (Bourriaud, 2002, p. 11). In the early twenty-first century, forms of communication using the Internet are pervasive, embedded in formally organised institutions and used sporadically in ephemeral groupings, including those of an artistic nature. Webcasting technologies have been available since the late 1990s, and interpersonal or group video-conferencing is now an established way for people to communicate and connect across great distances. Yet the application of these technologies to theatre performance remains nascent and companies exploring this technology work, for the most part, in uncharted territory. The emerging genre of camera-based Web performance often shares some of the codes and structures of film and cinema, but the interaction of physical performers and screened images using live video transmission is a hybrid form that requires sustained investigation if practitioners and critics are to exploit and understand fully its possibilities.

The recent work of Station House Opera, founded and led by director/ deviser Julian Maynard Smith, is significant because it has explored consistently the potential of telematic networked performance. *Live From Paradise* (2004), a co-production with Dutch company De Daders, used Webcast technology to connect performances in three apartments in the city of Amsterdam. *Play On Earth* (2006) developed a narrative that was played out trans-continentally in São Paulo, Newcastle Gateshead and Singapore. *The Other Is You* links three physical spaces: NP3 (a former school in Groningen), The Basement in Brighton, and the West German Gallery in Berlin.

Thematically and formally, *The Other Is You* is a departure from the narrative dramatic structure of Station House Opera's earlier telematic performances as the content and aesthetic concerns of this work model, rather than represent, everyday life. Thus the ordinary daily activities of people conducting similar actions in far away places take on deeper significance as they resonate across time and space. This project extends Station House Opera's explorations of how space – in particular non-theatrical and, more recently, virtual space – can be employed in performance. While the work is innovative and highly original, we will see that it reflects a tradition of spectacular events based on technology that dates back to the early years of the last century.

It might be helpful here to mention a point of terminology that Station House Opera use. They find the term 'persona', rather than 'character', more appropriate to describe the roles adopted by the performers. The use of 'persona' acknowledges current debates around character, persona and role in post-structuralist and postdramatic theatrical forms, such as *The Other Is You*. Maynard Smith eschewed the term 'character' and its associations, explaining 'we're not very interested in psychologically driven drama, and the idea of trying to make a point through characterisation and narrative.'[2] In the absence of narrative drive, it is the performed curiosity of each action that sustains interest in the situations presented.

Past events and current concerns

Station House Opera's work consistently challenges modes of reception, as was evident even in their inaugural performance, *Natural Disasters,* which suspended dramatic personae from bungee ropes in vertical space at the Acme Gallery, London, in 1980. Since then, the company has established a visually stimulating theatrical form in which space and location often function as dramatic agents, whilst also foregrounding the materiality of performance by drawing attention to objects and bodies located in specific spaces. Site-specificity and spectacle are recurrent features of the company's work; for instance, in *Drunken Madness* (1981) a potentially traumatic effect was created when performers were again suspended by ropes, this time dangling under the vertiginous Brooklyn Bridge. Station House Opera replace conventions of dramatic character with action-led performance registers; in *Piranesi in New York* (1988), for example, the performers grafted a shifting scenography of stairways, arches and towers, comprising some 3000 breeze blocks, onto the surface of the Brooklyn Bridge.

The company's propensity to push perceptual parameters has not been constrained by staging work in more conventional performance settings. When they create work in theatres, they extend the boundaries of conventional theatrical spaces into areas not originally intended for performance, such as backstage areas or front-of-house foyers. For example, *Roadmetal Sweetbread* (1998) employs projected playback video to follow a male persona from the avenues and alleyways outside whichever theatre building hosts the production, into that building and through its access corridors and backstage spaces, until he finally enters the conventional space of theatrical performance, the stage defined by its proscenium arch. (A version of this can be seen in a DVD recording of the production, available through Artsadmin, 2003.) These actions encourage the spectator to draw on their recollection of entering the theatre and to reflect on the role of space and memory in apprehending performance. As we will see, this metatheatrical dimension in which personae pass fluidly between actual physical spaces and two-dimensional virtual spaces, and in which performance occurs in non-theatrical spaces, also features in *The Other Is You.*

The Other Is You is fundamentally site-specific, extending the limits of physical performance spaces in each venue by incorporating virtual spaces represented by screens. For example, the physical space seen by the spectator in Brighton closely resembles the physical spaces in Holland and Germany; this effect is produced by space configuration, by camera angles and perspectives that give the illusion that the spaces on screen are just beyond the physical stage, as though glimpsed through a window. As with many of Station House Opera's media-driven works, *The Other Is You* challenges the fundamental immediacy of the theatrical present, supplementing the now-time of live action with the delay-time of video streamed to and from three remote locations.

The Other Is You revisits and extends territory first explored during the late 1960s and early 1970s, a period that also saw video technologies integrated into live performance for the first time. Artists including Mary Miss, Alice Aycock, Vito Acconci and Richard Serra produced media-driven work that interrogated notions of materiality, site-specificity, multiplicity, immediacy and post-linear temporality. These practitioners used contemporary video technologies, notably Sony's Porta-pack, to examine new combinations of virtual and actual spaces, producing hybrid forms that challenged notions of presence and foregrounded the apprehension of time and present-*ness*. However, interactions between live performance and projected images in vaudeville date back to the early twentieth century. As I examine more closely in *Music, Sound and Multimedia* (Kelly, 2007), *Gertie the Dinosaur* (1914) offers an example of intermediality in which an animated image is projected onto a cyclorama and appears to interact with her trainer and creator, Windsor McCay.

Contemporary multimedia theatre employing similar intermedial devices and aesthetics tends to eschew the pretence that it is something other than performance; instead it fully displays its artifices, technologies and framing devices. The interaction between live bodies and projected images produces a condition identified by Phaedra Bell as 'inter-media exchange', in which there is a 'mutual acknowledgement of images … interchange of glance, attribute or equipment … so that elements of the communication process cohere' (Bell, 2000, p. 44). We see this in *The Other Is You*, where performers in Holland, Germany and the UK seem to interact with one another in virtual and actual spaces. In one scene, for example, a virtual suitcase passes across the screens and the sequence culminates with an actual suitcase being dropped into the space in Brighton. There are also points where aspects of the *mise-en-scène* in each of the locations appear to cohere: for example when three personae, one in each space, sit at a table, holding their hands to their faces in a similar way (Figure 1).

Like other technology-driven work, *The Other Is You* strives to create a condition of telepresence, which Brenda Laurel defines as, 'a medium that allows you to take your body … into some other environment', which 'may be a computer-generated environment … a camera-originated environment, or … a combination of the two' (quoted in Coyle, 1993, p. 162). In *The Other Is You*, the environment is principally camera-originated as the camera operator plays a fundamental role, framing the action for transmission and reception onto a triptych of screens mounted onto a wall upstage of the performers.

Figure 1   Visual cohesion of action: all of the Bs sitting at a table during rehearsal, October 2006. Photo by Jem Kelly.

The streamed video triptych, in which Groningen appears on the left, Brighton in the centre and Berlin to the right, allows personae in each location to interact, but the two-dimensionality of the screened images is a constant reminder of their physical absence.

Unlike conventional modes of drama driven by conflict, by the wilfulness of characters and their differentiations, *The Other Is You* presents a model for living that celebrates connected-ness. This situates the performance alongside contemporary 'relational' artworks that are concerned more with 'states of encounter' and 'the invention of the everyday and the development of time lived' than with representations of character and specific cultural/social contexts (Bourriaud, 2002, p. 14). *The Other Is You* is formed by the sense of time lived, and framed by the idea that technology can re-locate us spatially: the delay between the physical actions in the stage performance and the screened video images, caused by the Internet time lag, keeps the spectator continuously aware of these aspects of time and space. The state of encounter is tripartite, as the audience in each of the three spaces watch what the performers are doing on the stage

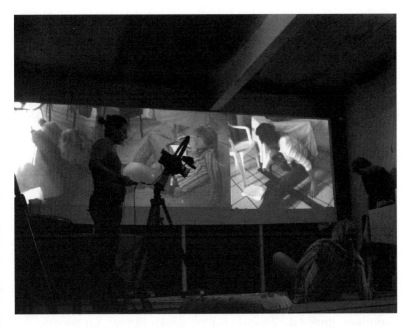

Figure 2   Performers in each space are framed by the camera. Photo by Jem Kelly.

in front of them and onscreen, whilst mindful that others are also watching physical action in remote locations. The Mexican wave that preceded the performance I attended demonstrates the relational propensity of audience members, shaping the state of encounter as one of interaction and temporal delay.

In performance, however, cohesion of vision is only partial, as each audience perceives different perspectives of the live and screened action. Yet this also creates multiple elements that compete for the spectator's attention, enabling a degree of agency in which the spectator chooses where to look and how to read the action. The performers in the remote spaces remain physically inaccessible, despite actions in each of the spaces appearing to cohere onscreen: they are out of place and temporally displaced in relation to the local event. This contravenes a key element of theatre performance – the physical co-presence of audience and performer – which is evident in only one quarter of the elements comprising the performance system of screens and action. Nonetheless, *The Other Is You* sustains its engagement by building a sense of connection, spatially, virtually and in perceived action. Eschewing linear narrative, the performance emphasises visual similarities in the three spaces that enable connections to be made through a combination of gestural signs, task-based actions, costume and proxemics. Many of the signs are mimetic of everyday action – reading a newspaper, walking to a door, drinking a glass of wine – so that the spectator engages viscerally and vicariously in the actions performed.

The performance encounter also stimulates the spectator's imagination, as not all of the spaces are discernible. This reflects Maynard Smith's intention that the individual and local are but parts of a larger global picture:

> We're all engaged in a worldwide performance, but we're not really aware of all the other parts of it. It's as often been a factor in our work that the 'bigger things' haven't been tightly constructed with only one view in mind, one sort of strict perspective.[3]

The Other Is You does not produce a metanarrative in which all global behaviour is unified, but presents instead specific situations in which performers undertake actions that are similar but remain open to different interpretations. The varying visual perspectives offered on these actions work, paradoxically, against unification whilst enabling connections to be drawn between physical actions of human behaviour and the situations in which they are carried out.

The devising processes

In terms of creative process, a fascinating aspect of this project concerns the relationship and interaction between the three teams operating simultaneously in Groningen, Brighton and Berlin. Devising *The Other Is You* presented particular challenges for its three directors, Maynard Smith, Martin Clausen and Floris Van Delft, not least because Clausen and Van Delft became part of the company for this project only. The fact that the three directors had their own technical teams, performers and ideas raised practical and philosophical issues, which were overcome in part by using Internet technology to discuss creative ideas and to view what was taking place in each location.

The technical set-up is replicated in each location and operates as follows. Video is streamed from a single camera in each space using the Darwin Quick Time system (this is employed only to transmit because it contains error correction that could produce packet loss, resulting in loss of image quality if used in reception mode). The video signals are streamed from each space to a server in Holland and are then relayed to each of the spaces, and anywhere on the Internet, as multicast images. The Dutch server is used to keep the images synchronised, so that all the performers appear to move at the same time on the screens. However, there is a two-second delay from transmission to reception of the video images; this produces an odd effect, as the spectator sees the performers move physically in the space and two seconds later observes the same movements on screen. Thus the spectator is able to predict, to some extent, what will be seen on the screens and also to see what has taken place in the remote locations.

Bringing different spaces into a state of visual cohesion proved extremely complex and required precise organisation. Although the devising period began with a week-long period of meetings and workshops in Berlin that involved all three directors, from that point on the directors had no unmediated face-to-face communication. During the five-week devising period, video technologies were used for visual communication and Skype for instantaneous audio instruction, comment and discussion between the spaces, while email allowed a work-plan to be sent that would help shape daily activity. In performance, the performers are given cues from Brighton via Skype, which allows for instantaneous audio communication between the locations. Owing to the difficulty in devising with technology, relationships within this process were structured in a relatively hierarchical way and I will argue that the process was akin to a form of collaborative *auteurship*.

The work undertaken during the devising period was very much to do with the planning, the preparation, the research, and figuring out how the ideas presented by Maynard Smith would be realised in each country. This way of working had as much to do with the way the performance was funded as with directorial control. *The Other Is You* was financed through a European initiative, Culture 2000. As Maynard Smith explains: 'It is an incredibly complex project to set up, just to find venues and teams of people who can all free themselves up at the same time. The actual business, the logistics of it are really nightmarish.'[4] The company located producers or producing venues in the various locations who were able to provide the infrastructure for the project. These producers or venues then recommended directors who they thought would be 'amenable or interested or open to the idea',[5] although these directors, Clausen and Van Delft, had had little experience of working with multimedia. Neither of them had previously worked with Station

House Opera, although Clausen had seen some of Maynard Smith's telematic work before. (Clausen's background is eclectic, using a variety of approaches including dance, devising, site-specific, text-based and live art with companies such as Sophiensæle, HAU, Tanzfabrik, Lajos Talamonti, Nico and the Navigators, Gob Squad and his own, Two Fish, while Van Delft trained in directing at the Amsterdam Theatre School.) Nor was Maynard Smith able to see the finished performance spaces in Groningen and Berlin. The costs of such a technologically complex project limited the time for bringing the whole thing together to just five weeks. Maynard Smith reflects on how these factors affected the content of the work:

> There was a limited amount of contact time with the directors in the other locations, and none [with] the actors in the other locations. I spent a week with the other directors in Berlin ... but it was one week of going through very, very basic ideas. The other directors had busy schedules, and so there was a limited amount of real working together. I would have much preferred it if we'd had a much longer rehearsal time to really get to grips with the actual substance of the piece.[6]

During the week of face-to-face communication between the three directors, they experimented with the notion of the three screens on laptops, made short videos and, as Van Delft puts it, 'had long conversations where everyone wanted something different'. Van Delft emphasises that the three 'weren't trying to get on the same line of thinking – the takes were very different'.[7]

Once rehearsals started, each team had a daily period of working separately before coming together with the other teams via technology. The daily rehearsal/devising sessions were extremely well organised – as they had to be, given the complexity of communicating and synchronising activity across the three remote locations. Each day Maynard Smith would email or fax a pre-prepared work-plan to the other directors, sometimes amending this on the day of rehearsal to take into account points raised in their discussions. The daily scene list, or work-plan, would then be discussed with the performers, after which the ideas were tested with the performers and camera operators, and finally all three sets of performers would work together, communicating in audio via Skype and visually via the screens. There was thus some room for each of the directors to take independent approaches with their particular teams (directors also had control over casting), although the scope for this was limited.

Devising is usually a collaborative process that takes place in the same space, at the same time and often without a script. For Clausen, whose expertise is in physical theatre and who usually has 'no ideas or subject when I start a creation', this 'system of working with three places at the same time, the three continuous pictures, was quite demanding'.[8] Referring to his approach to some previous Station House Opera pieces, Maynard Smith says: 'you start in the rehearsal space with something and say "let's do this" and you realise that it doesn't work and then you thrash around and find something in the end which doesn't bear a lot of relation to it. But this particular piece, the basic form of it, existed from the very beginning.'[9]

Issues regarding the forms and content of *The Other Is You* led to many of the decisions being taken by Maynard Smith, whose artistic vision was informed by a knowledge of telematic performance. An example occurred one afternoon when the Internet connection went live and the director in Berlin announced that they were going to select costumes for the piece. A female performer in Groningen appeared in a yellow dress and a man entered the frame wearing a light-blue jacket. Although this costume had not been mentioned during the morning discussions, and Maynard Smith was unprepared for it, he observed that the colours were not appropriate if the image was to be legible and advised that: 'it's the wrong shade of blue. ... It has to be a bolder, darker blue.'[10]

Clausen was happy to follow Maynard Smith's lead as: 'he had all the experience, and so we asked him to teach us how it works.'[11] Van Delft, though, was more intent on contributing his own ideas to the creative process rather than following a homogeneous process: 'I think also that there had to be three different processes. In my own case, I would put a storyline, kind of directed scenes, which were about relationships.'[12] As will become apparent, Van Delft's approach was at odds with that taken by Maynard Smith and the Brighton-based performers, who were interested in role-play and non-matrixed performance. This highlights one of the problems with a devising process in which different directors were hundreds of miles apart. Not only could nuances be lost, but basic tenets of the devising process could be overlooked. In fact, Van Delft introduced an additional performer, a commentator figure who did not appear on the screen and of whom Maynard Smith was unaware.

Scope for the performers to engage in collaborative creation was perhaps even more limited. Maynard Smith explains:

When we started rehearsals, we had ideas that we rehearsed in a fairly basic form. And of course the performers had had space to find what things to do within that. Somehow running counter to that a bit, is that they had to understand that they would be interacting in whatever they did. ... Work[ing] independently of the other locations every day ... we had a chance of exploring things without the technical and conceptual complications of being online. So in a sense we explored stuff ... but they also had to be aware that ... the sort of interesting thing about the performance is that you have some kind of relationship with these people who are not there, so it's hard to play in a kind of free and easy sort of way.[13]

This explains the tension in the devising process between the performer's impulse to spontaneous action and improvisation and the need to be aware of what *might* result in action that was co-ordinated with absent performers. During the afternoons of rehearsals, the ideas developed in the morning could be shared, discussed and tested with the performers in other locations. But interactions between them via the video images on the screens were not always straightforward, as Zoë Bouras, a performer in the Brighton space, observes:

> The camera became the device through which my performance persona could connect with the others. The potential of this portal ... was a piece of technological trickery requiring impeccable timing, both human and machine. We relied on technology to keep us together in three places, but, with a two-to-twenty second delay on visuals and intermittent Internet breakdowns, rehearsals were tricky.
>
> (Bouras, 2007, p. 21)

As the process was basically the same for each day of the devising period, I will illustrate the methods used by referring principally to one day of devising.

At 11 am on the morning of 23 October 2006, three performers in Brighton – Bouras, Orion Maxted and Victoria Melody – attentively take notes along with production assistant Oliver Hymans, as Maynard Smith gives the following guidelines for how rehearsals will proceed:

> Depending on time, we'll have to do one and two as a sequence. The first set is three to five, the second set is six to eight and the last one eight to nine. We have to be fairly strict on [the] time we spend on stuff.[14]

Figure 3   Scene 4 starting point of 'Reptile Brain'. Photo by Jem Kelly.

These numbers represent precise subdivisions of a scene, in this case Scene 5, into smaller units of action (Figure 3) that are tested-out during the day. The scene, 'Reptile Brain', has been discussed amongst the directors between 10 am and 11 am, and will be tested-out until 1 pm, when the video streaming and projections are activated.

The discussion with the performers in Brighton begins with a description of the scenario as set out on the day's work-plan:

> A, B and C [the personae] each have a mental state, but it doesn't really affect their actions, which are mainly everyday. It is as if they are not aware of what they are doing. So, unaware as they are, they tend to trigger each other's behaviour: action triggers action. In between actions are long periods of inaction, so when an action occurs it comes as something of a surprise, and the fact it is triplicated is a greater surprise.[15]

The tone and tenor of the situation gives insight to the performance register adopted by the performers, illustrating how they will perform the proposed actions. They are invited to behave as though 'learning how to become human', which is intended to confer a sense of wonder when actions are performed and gives them an estranging effect when observed by the spectator.[16] I asked the performers if they could explain these instructions and whether they informed notions of character. Melody stressed that in order to behave as instructed, 'it's really important that we don't have characters, that we don't have back-stories.'[17] I remarked that the performers in each location are identified as A, B and C (they are also named: in Groningen, Ad, Bea and Chris; in Brighton, Aldo, Bernadette and Charlie; and in Berlin, Anton, Berta and Conrad, though these do not appear on the programme for the show), which would suggest characterisations of some kind are taking place. Maxted offered an explanation: 'You don't develop a character per se; there's a non-specific-ness, but something more universal. Our own personality might come through some of the ideas we're exploring.'[18]

This led me to suggest that the performance registers belonged somewhere along the 'continuum' of 'Not-Acting–Acting' categorised by Michael Kirby, and could in places be identified as non-matrixed performance in which the performers 'tended to "be" nobody or nothing other than themselves; nor ... represent, or pretend to be in, a time or place different from that of the spectator' (Kirby, 2002, p. 40). Bouras was familiar with Kirby's classification and situated the register as belonging to 'the persona that might appear quite low-down in the non-matrixed area'.[19] She went on to differentiate between the 'calculating element to C' that makes the Cs more akin to characters, whereas 'A and B have this sort of innocence that makes them feel very simple.'[20] In performance, the Cs show an awareness of actions performed by the As and Bs in the other countries, and all of the Cs are aware of each other and 'may be aware of the audience ... rather like an animal in a zoo might.'[21] In contrast, according to Melody, 'the As and Bs don't know anything, have no awareness.'[22]

In addition to the nine performers, there is a completely non-matrixed, 'not-acting' (Kirby, ibid.) performer in each of the three spaces: the camera operator, whose role is purely functional. The presence of the camera operator diffuses any sense that the performed behaviour is illusory, as does the time-delay on the screened images, and these factors lend the event a reflexivity: the spectators never lose sight of the fact that they are watching a performance. Additionally, the cameras allow the physical spaces to be extended by providing views outside those spaces. At the beginning of the performance, the cameras in each location 'are leaving the building, getting as far as the video cable allows'.[23] There appears to be a *cinema verité* approach, as cameras 'should be empty of human interest', an intention largely borne out as cameras provide descriptive shots, such as ascending stairs, going through doors, panning left and right to survey scenery.

Camera angles and shot-type also play a large part in determining the shape of the performance and the limits of action undertaken, as a description of a devised section of 'Reptile Brain' illustrates. The spaces in each geographical location, though slightly different, lack specificity as the walls and floors are painted white, although the work-plan identifies them as 'different rooms' that are simply furnished with 'tables' and some 'chairs'.[24] In Scene 4 of 'Reptile Brain', there is a table upstage right at which A (Maxted) sits reading a paper (Figure 4). In this section, 'Action is the same in all three spaces' and during performance each of the performers in all three locations receives in-ear audio cues from the stage manager in Brighton that enable them to move simultaneously so that screened action is synchronised.[25] In this rehearsal Maynard Smith takes the performers through the cues, and at cue 4a (Figure 5), persona A (Maxted) closes the newspaper he is holding, places it on the table and moves his head forward. This

Figure 4 A sits reading a paper. Photo by Jem Kelly.

Figure 5   A closes paper as C stands up. Photo by Jem Kelly.

movement brings his head into the frame of the camera, producing a medium close-up on the centre screen, whilst C can be seen in long-shot sitting at a table downstage left. At cue 4b persona C (Bouras) stands up, walks around the table and past the open doorway (situated at stage left) and waits (Figure 6: Bouras can be seen on the centre screen walking past the doorway). At cue 4c, B (Melody) walks to the table (downstage left, Figure 7), sits down and places her hands to her head (Figure 8 and Figure 2).

During rehearsal, the first run-through is effective, but Maynard Smith points out that in performance the sequence must flow without interruption and that the cues are 'linked directly to each other'.[26] Cues 5a, b and c require A (Maxted) to look over his shoulder, look back to the table and then move out of shot. Cues 6a and b see first B (Melody) then C (Bouras) look up at the ceiling, then down again. At cue 7a, B (Melody) stands up, walks to the door (stage left), looks through it then returns to sit at the table. Cue 7b sees A (Maxted) walk diagonally across the stage, look out of the door and remain standing. Cue 7b sees C (Bouras) walk around the table and stand.

As can be seen from the above sequence, the performed actions are tightly choreographed, as is the camera angle, shot-type and

Figure 6 B walks to table ... . Photo by Jem Kelly.

Figure 7 B sits down. Photo by Jem Kelly.

movement (Figure 9). Maynard Smith is exacting about the precise positions of the performers during rehearsal, which leaves little room for improvisation in the conventional sense.

Figure 8   C approaches table. Photo by Jem Kelly.

Figure 9   Maynard Smith directs camera tracking. Photo by Jem Kelly.

The performers in each of the three locations must adhere to the cues so that the actions remain synchronised on the screens, but also be aware of where the camera is at all times so that perspectives are not interrupted. The field of vision offered to the spectator from each space is limited to the camera position, but the spectator can decide where to look and when. Also, the different perspectives make the images on the screens seem less predictable (Figure 10), which forces the spectators to configure their comprehension of each of the spaces by using their imaginations.

I asked Maynard Smith whether, given the technical complexities of the project, the entire experience had to be shaped to some extent autocratically in order for *The Other Is You* to make visual sense, to cohere. He replied

Ultimately, there's a kind of uneasy balance between what happens live in each location as a show – as a performance for a direct audience – and what is broadcast on the screens as a sort of making up

Figure 10 The afternoon rehearsal of 'Reptile Brain', showing different camera perspectives. Photo by Jem Kelly.

a triptych of images which work together. That's a very complicated relationship. ... Time is a big issue and in a way it might have been better if we'd had a much more scripted piece, but we did try to devise it online to a largish degree.[27]

Implicit in this response is Maynard Smith's acknowledgement that devising 'online' is very problematic, owing to the gaps in communication produced by the physical absence of two-thirds of the company for much of the time. However, visual cohesion is arrived at in performance via the screened images, and Clausen emphasised the fact that the camera movement was 'very much scripted' and that that element of the 'script' was '80 per cent coming from Brighton'.[28] Thus, owing to constraints of time and finance, and to the absence of physical proximity of everyone involved in devising *The Other Is You*, the methodology reified in practice is akin to *auteur* theory.

This proposal is not without its problems when considering devised practice, which is usually thought of as a collaborative process, and in the light of postmodern theories, which refute notions of authorship. In his paper 'The Death of the Author', post-structuralist thinker Roland Barthes articulated problems of tracing authorial intentions and their being realised and read faithfully by the spectator (Barthes, 1977, p. 142). With Barthes' essay, the analytical balance shifts away from production to reception theory, in which the reader becomes the co-writer, the co-author of meaning. Despite this, *auteur* theory remains useful in helping comprehend how devising processes can take on different outcomes when elements of one performance are undertaken by independent operators in different locations. On one level, *The Other Is You* is generated principally by the ideas of Maynard Smith, and so he could be considered the author of the work (except for differences that occurred in the realisation of the performances in each space, which were beyond his control).

To reflect the situation in which different contributors realise their own intentions, Berys Grant identifies a collaborative mode of film *auteurship* – 'multiple authorship' – in which there are 'many authors ... plausibly occupying some or all of the main production roles' (Grant, 1999, p. 152). This casts light on the devising process of *The Other Is You*, in which differing intentions in each of the locations gave rise to variance in what took place. Although Maynard Smith remained 'in overall control of the combined image' that appeared on the screens, there were other, unforeseen elements occurring in the physical spaces.[29] I would argue that the process positions Maynard Smith as the main, or dominant collaborator, owing as much to his organisational role as to his creative intentions, some of which were not realised fully. There remain elements of variation in the process. These included differences produced by space and performers, but more important was the fact that there could be different responses to Maynard Smith's aims by Clausen and Van Delft, both of whom had their own intentions and preferences. Despite this, *The Other Is You* obtained a remarkable cohesion in the action depicted on the screens, a factor that militated against the attenuation of Maynard Smith's ideas for the overall reception of the performance.

Conclusion

The relational encounter of *The Other Is You* (and, I would argue, a reason for its success) is to position spectators in a place of contemplation centred on the differences, similarities and materialities of actual and virtual spaces. This condition is set up from the beginning, as the performance proper commences with the camera operators pursuing the physically present performers in each space on a journey to the building they will temporarily inhabit. This journey is significant as it also marks the passage from actual space to virtual space in each of the geographical locations. In Brighton, the journey is defined by a carefully coiled video cable unfurling on the floor as the camera operator moves from the staging area through an access corridor and clangs up a set of steel stairs. There is a vertiginous moment as the physical body of the camera operator disappears from view, causing the spectator's gaze to shift from the empty corridor to the screen, from the actual to the virtual space. However, a tangible link to the virtual realm is sustained in a curious way by the video cable, which continues to unfurl in actual space on the concrete floor. I was tempted to reach out and grab the cable, if only to prove that I retained the potential for physical intervention in the event, and it is this sense of possible agency that charges the performance: we feel that we could reach out and affect the physical, and by so doing alter the virtual. Outside in the street and growing onscreen, a vehicle rapidly approaches the camera and its presence is felt as sound and vibration in the rumbling walls of the basement: the van is just to stage right, somewhere beyond the ceiling.

By beginning in this way, *The Other Is You* introduces an intense engagement in the materiality of the theatrical event that is sustained across the performance because of the disparity apprehended in the physical presence of the actual and the delayed-liveness of the virtual. The just-within-reach-ness of the physically present performers is tempered by the just-out-of-reach-ness of the virtual performers, who are always slightly late in their movements. In the action-driven performance, infused with attitudes and emotions embodied by the performers, we encounter modes of being in three locations that are connected not through narrative but through the interrelations and disjunctions of material and immaterial presences.

Memory is fundamental to our appreciation of what is apprehended in watching *The Other Is You*. Physical actions are observed to cohere with screened images, but the temporal delay unsettles our certainty of recollection in the short term. Henri Bergson's description of what he terms the 'psychical ... present' seems particularly pertinent to describing a perceptual mode in which the spectator must be mindful of 'the immediate past' and a 'determination of the immediate future' (Bergson, 1991, p. 138). *The Other Is You* demands new and intense roles of expectation, of anticipation and of recollection, both for the spectators – who must spot the differences between what is observed on stage, what they will see on screen and how this resembles what they recollect – and for the performers, who must be mindful of three locations and extensions of persona simultaneously. The performers interrelate with each other as intended, 'performing with a physical body and with an extension, manifest by others in remote locations'.[30] But as the performers do not employ conventional means of communication, the spectator is forced to compute similarities of actions performed – not verbally, but visually – in actual and virtual *mises-en-scene,* or suffer a crisis of misrecognition.

Bergson refers to the twin action of memory, 'covering ... with a cloak of recollections a core of immediate perception, and also contracting a number of external moments' (p. 51). *The Other Is You* extends this duality by making the just-past visually observable alongside the now-time of the present. For Bergson, memory and duration enable the 'conservation *and* preservation of the past in the present' (p. 51); by re-presenting perspectives of the past in the theatrical present as image, however, *The Other Is You* transforms memory into a triple mode of address in the apprehension of present actions, of re-lived experiences and the looped re-presentations of delayed-liveness.

Chronology of selected productions

Play On Earth, an international collaboration performed simultaneously in Brazil, England and Singapore. Performed as part of the World Summit on Arts & Culture in Newcastle Gateshead in June 2006.

Live From Paradise, a collaboration with Dutch theatre company, De Daders. Performed simultaneously in three locations in Amsterdam. National and international tours 2004–5.

Mare's Nest, a play about double, triple and quadruple lives interacting virtually and physically. National and international tour 2001.

Roadmetal Sweetbread, a performance for two performers and a video. National and international tour 1998.

Notes

1. Flyer for *The Other Is You,* Artsadmin, 2006.
2. Julian Maynard Smith, interview with the author, April 2007.
3. Ibid.
4. Ibid.
5. Ibid.
6. Ibid.
7. Floris Van Delft, interview with the author, April 2007.
8. Martin Clausen, interview with the author, April 2007.
9. Maynard Smith, interview with the author, April 2007.
10. Maynard Smith, digital video of working practice recorded by the author, 23 October 2009.
11. Clausen, interview with the author, April 2007.
12. Floris Van Delft, interview with the author, April 2007.
13. Maynard Smith, interview with the author, April 2007.
14. Maynard Smith, digital video of working practice recorded by the author, 23 October 2009.
15. Work-plan courtesy of Julian Maynard-Smith.
16. Maynard Smith, digital video of working practice recorded by the author, 23 October 2009.
17. Victoria Melody, interview with the author, 23 October 2006.
18. Orion Maxted, interview with the author, 23 October 2006.
19. Zoë Bouras, interview with the author, 23 October 2006.
20. Ibid.
21. Notes from Julian Maynard Smith.
22. Victoria Melody, interview with the author, 23 October 2006.
23. Maynard Smith, taken from production notes.
24. Maynard Smith, digital video of working practice recorded by the author, 23 October 2009.
25. Work-plan courtesy of Julian Maynard Smith.
26. Maynard Smith, digital video of working practice recorded by the author, 23 October 2009.
27. Maynard Smith, interview with the author, April 2007.
28. Clausen, interview with the author, April 2007.
29. Maynard Smith, Interview with the author, April 2007.
30. Ibid.

3
The Making of Faulty Optic's *Dead Wedding*
Inertia, Chaos and Adaptation

Tim Moss

It is difficult to faithfully record and disseminate the process of a company devising a piece of theatre, to excavate those 'ephemeral moments of devised performance' (Govan, Nicholson and Normington, 2007, p. 9). It is impossible to watch the company in every minute of their process: you are not privy to their dreams; you are not with them as they overhear a conversation on a bus; you are outside fetching the tea at the very moment that they make a breakthrough in the devising process because a bird has flown through an open window, causing them to think of the next scene as a pair of wings fluttering hysterically. But it is possible to tell *something* of the truth if certain moments are allowed to encapsulate it, to stand as small parts of the larger metaphor that will act as a simulacrum of the reality of performance devising. Then it is possible to give an account of the difficult, delirious, funny, frustrating and joyful process that theatre and performance artists undergo as they make work. Rather than write the whole story of the making of *Dead Wedding* I will look at certain significant moments, trusting that they contain and explain the fashion in which this remarkable performance came into being.

I will use a playful analogy called Chaotic Darwinism to help describe and understand Faulty Optic's devising process: the analogy is a combination of a Darwinian idea on natural selection and the study of patterns of 'chaos' in Chaos Theory. I posit the idea that some of Faulty Optic's ideas survive because they are able to adapt to the changing circumstances of the creative process, while retaining their relevance. Others are born out of 'chaos' and Chaos Theory shows us that chaotic systems create enough instability in a process to disrupt usual patterns of behaviour, which results in a new order emerging. In this way they can be described as creative systems and creativity is at the heart of what is being described in this chapter: how the members of Faulty Optic accessed and employed their creativity in the making of *Dead Wedding*.

Faulty Optic, which receives core funding from Arts Council England and support for international touring from the British Council, has been making works for over 20 years, having been founded in 1987 by Gavin Glover and Liz Walker. The company is based in Holmfirth, West Yorkshire, and is often described as a puppet performance company, but it is significant that Faulty Optic's website describes the company's work as 'Theatre of Animation',[1] eschewing a straightforward reference to puppetry, which too simplistically pigeonholes its work. The company has developed its work to include many other elements, and a quotation from its artistic policy on the British Council website best describes the milieu in which it operates: it 'combines visual and physical theatre and puppetry with an exploration of 3D film animation, automata and mechanical sculpture to create a unique style of theatre'.[2] It continues to 'create exciting collaborations with other artists and to experiment with different artforms'.[3] This combining of mediums and theatrical styles places Faulty Optic alongside companies such as IOU and Slung Low Theatre Company (in some of the latter's installation performance work), who often adopt long, intricate patterns of devising, rather than a model of performers working intensively in a studio for a shorter burst of creative activity. The former pattern is in part necessitated by their use of newly wrought technical and sculptural apparatus as central performance elements.

Faulty Optic's previous work, much of it still in the company's performance repertoire, contains macabre humour, evident not just within its shows' narratives and thematic content (there is often a preoccupation with death) but in the sets and puppets themselves; Faulty Optic has won the *Observer* newspaper award for 'most macabre puppets'.[4] The titles of some of its shows prior to *Dead Wedding* also reflect this sensibility: *Darwin's Dead Herring, Snuffhouse Dustlouse, Soiled, Licked, Horsehead* (which conjures up the famous grotesque image from Francis Ford Coppola's first *Godfather* film). Faulty Optic's puppetry background was established in their work at the Little Angel Marionette Theatre in London in the mid-1980s, and Glover and Walker have since combined their puppeteering prowess and considerable making skills with an interest in other art forms to create darkly humorous performance work.

Apart from *Horsehead,* which was made in 2005 and included a narrator figure, the company's work before *Dead Wedding* had historically used few words, allowing it to leapfrog language barriers, and this has helped to facilitate its touring profile. It has performed extensively throughout Britain and in most of Western Europe as well as in Canada, North and South America and Indonesia. Glover and Walker remain as the core of the company and have a clear vision for the direction of their work, but have collaborated with other performers, puppeteers, musicians, composers, lighting and sound designers, and automata and film makers. *Dead Wedding* was a collaborative project, but as Glover and Walker suggest, not like any other collaboration that they had undertaken previously.

Dead Wedding was officially commissioned in March 2006 by Opera North projects director Dominic Gray, and the Manchester International Festival (MIF), for performance at the Library Theatre in Manchester in July 2007. The terms of the commission required the work to be a collaboration between Faulty Optic and a composer/musician approved by the commissioners. This was the first difference from the fashion in which Faulty Optic previously approached collaborative work: 'usually we choose to collaborate with people whose work we know quite well. ... Collaboration tends to happen organically through conversation and the sharing of ideas.'[5] But this time they had actively to seek a musician and have their choice approved by Opera North.

Although commissioned in 2006 the project had been talked about 'two or three years before',[6] so the seed of the idea had probably been sown in late 2004. Walker says that 'Originally, I think he [Dominic Gray] wanted to do a festival around the theme of the Underworld ... and we thought it was going to be a much smaller project.'[7] So the project had a three-year gestation period before finally being born at the Manchester International Festival, but the child of this union had irregular growth spurts and twisted and mutated a number of times before its birth, and even then shifted its identity over a number of performances. Perhaps, like humans, its identity was never fixed but liable to change as and when circumstances demand.

Dead Wedding was part of Opera North's celebration of the 400th anniversary of Monteverdi's *Orfeo*, which in its time was itself an experimental piece of musical writing and one of the first that could be described as opera. Opera North described *Dead Wedding* as 'a contemporary re-telling of the Orpheus myth'.[8] In the original story, Eurydice is killed by a snake's bite soon after her marriage to Orpheus, and is transported to Hades, where the dead reside under the careful watch of Pluto, king of the Underworld. Orpheus descends into Hades, and singing in his extraordinary voice pleads with Pluto to let Eurydice live a while longer. Pluto is so moved by the beauty of Orpheus' singing that he agrees to let Eurydice leave, on condition that Orpheus refrains from looking back at her as the newlyweds ascend from the underworld. When they have almost reached the world of the living, Orpheus forgets himself and glances back, permanently consigning Eurydice to Hades. A grief stricken Orpheus is then torn limb from limb. However, *Dead Wedding* is not a re-telling or re-imagining of this myth but a sequel to it, imagining another meeting of the two ill-fated lovers when both are dead, waiting to pass into the deeper regions of the extensive kingdom of Hades.

* * *

It is 5 July 2006 when I first meet Glover and Walker to negotiate the disturbance of watching their process. An email from Glover gives a sense of the workshop and rehearsal space where most of the practical work on *Dead Wedding* takes place:

> it is tucked up a track at the side of a mill ... beware of forklifts, giant bales, scrap industrial bits ... take care not to run any wandering poultry over. ... The workshop is the Old Canteen, a 70s one storey building between the end of the mill and a field.[9]

The workshop is many things: a storage space filled with materials such as foam, cloth, latex, wood and metal; a tool store; a rehearsal space with a basic, movable lighting setup; a film studio with contraptions for holding cameras to assist in the making of animated film. There are various delineated spaces within the workshop dedicated to the multifarious tasks of making a performance, and over the course of the time that I visit the workshop they change their function: the puppet-making vestibule becomes an editing suite and the set-construction space morphs into a rehearsal room.

Walking in for the first time I interrupt them in the act of making. Walker is busy adjusting and adapting the body of the puppet that will eventually represent Orpheus, while Glover takes off his welding mask and stops piecing together a preliminary piece of set. They clear tools and papers from a table, dust down some chairs, and we drink black coffee and eat biscuits as we talk about how this observation might work. I stress that I want to be as unobtrusive as possible. Walker says that I will probably be roped in to do things and to make comments about what I see. Glover tells me that they do not usually work with a director but in the process of making a show they both step out from time to time to give an outside eye to the work, and they have other trusted friends and acquaintances whose opinions they canvass. They point to a large mirror that stands at the side of the main space of the workshop which they use to monitor the action of their work. I imagine a puppet ballet class with puppet pliés and pirouettes. We talk about their approach to making a show and ascertain that they do not imagine themselves having a particularly fixed process that they apply to making work. They joke that it will be interesting for them to find out how it is that they do make work, as it is not something that has previously concerned them.

At this point I take stock of what progress has already been made towards realising *Dead Wedding*. There is a firm commission, a performance date to work towards and funding in place. There is a possible collaborator who might work on the musical soundscape, but this has not been finalised. Their first choice musical collaborator has been rejected because he is not well known enough to the commissioners. Glover and Walker imagine that they will both be the puppeteers in the performance, and they have begun work on ideas for puppets, including some initial fabrication. They have also built a nascent set for the show. I am shown scribbles of design on scraps of paper and a typed initial scenario that includes possible characters, sets and actions, along with ideas for sound effects/music/mood, lighting and film.

It is important to note that this written scenario does not constitute a conventional playscript. It is a set of possible actions for the puppets but, just as importantly, it is also a guide towards what needs to be fabricated in terms of set and other sculptural objects. Beside each scene are comments such as 'Melodramatic', 'Cruel but funny' and 'Beautiful'.[10] For Faulty Optic, mood is an important guiding principle. The desired emotional impact is as much of a starting point for devising performance as a set of possible actions. This made particular sense in the case of *Dead Wedding*: they imagined that a musical collaborator would want to know what the desired emotional resonance of the sound should be for each sequence of the piece. This premonition of what a collaborator might need proved welcomingly prescient and absolutely vital when a composer was finally attached to the project at a relatively late stage in the process.

At this first meeting I talk with Glover and Walker about IOU (also based in West Yorkshire and with whom I worked as a performer–deviser in the 1990s), suggesting that there are similarities in some of the ways each company begins the process of making work and also in the ways that they do not begin to make work. Neither company begins with a scripted text that forms the architecture or the scaffolding for the piece. Both companies begin with a strong emphasis on the design or visual content of the performance, or a theme that might serve as a foundation upon which to build (rather than a pattern to follow). Walker and Glover indicate that I can have open access to their process but suggest that there will be periods of time when nothing interesting will happen. However, I leave our first meeting feeling that it is important to see the non-interesting periods of inertia as much as the interesting leaps forward. It is useful to see that forward progress is not always easy when devising performance, not least so that other practitioners and students of performance can take heart that they are not alone in the one step forward, two steps sideways, backwards or down a cul-de-sac that is often the reality of performance making.

Two weeks later, I receive another email from Walker:

> June 15 script is now out of date (a bit), the current one is scribbled in our note book. ... We have been building a preliminary set with help from Matt – a very keen set builder from Leeds. I can't keep up with him! We have met a graduate – Leah – who may help with the animation over the summer. We don't yet have confirmation from [name deleted] – the musician/composer. We may be looking yet again for someone else soon.[11]

People are being added to the collaborative mix and in August I meet Leah Morgan, a graduate in art and design, who helps to make the animated films that are an integral part of the performance. At this meeting there's a discussion between Walker, Glover and Morgan: the filmed sections of the performance will represent aspects of the Underworld, and focus on the pennies used by dead souls for payment of the journey across the River Styx into Hades. They also decide that this month they will build some set and play with animation ideas but they must also resuscitate their previous production, *Horsehead*, for an autumn tour. This will involve re-rehearsals and an extended time away from their home base, so little practical work can now happen on *Dead Wedding* until late November 2006.

At this point it becomes evident that this show is not going to be made using a conventional working model that might see the assembly of the show's participants, followed by their working together over a fixed and continuous period, culminating in the performance of the work. Indeed, this idea of a conventional model may be a red herring. As Heddon and Milling stress, devising processes 'are fluid. Moreover they are located in specific times and places. In light of this it becomes problematic and disingenuous to propose the existence of "models"' (Heddon and Milling, 2006, p. 78). This Faulty Optic process proceeds in a stop–start fashion: there is some playing with half-finished puppets, a look at the possibilities of film, then more set construction, followed by a two-month layoff for touring and running workshops, followed by ... what? In summer 2006 no one is completely sure. But the show is not due to open for another 11 months. This is the calm before the metaphorical storm that will unleash a measure of chaos into the proceedings, which in turn will determine the route to the show's construction.

I have one more meeting with the company in October before a type of 'chaos' starts to feed back into the system of this creative process. In the workshop, Glover, Walker and Morgan are stealing some time between *Horsehead* tour dates to try out ideas for filmed material. They are working on a section where Orpheus will remember the terrible climactic moment when he foolishly looks back at Eurydice as he walks out of Hades, in direct contravention of Pluto's instructions. This section will be a recurring moment of anguished memory for Orpheus shown through film but as Glover says, 'looking round isn't particularly dramatic.'[12] Walker remembers the moment when they decided upon the action that would show Orpheus' memory of his dreadful mistake: they imagined the scene as a race to leave Hades, set in a cavernous athletics stadium. They 'wanted that empty feeling' and 'hadn't twigged that it was like the Olympics,'[13] the Olympics being born in Ancient Greece, connecting with the original myth in terms of place and epoch. And from 'somewhere' they decided that the image of Eurydice's face would be seen on a television screen and that the television would wheel around the track after Orpheus, both of them running the race to leave Hades (Figure 11).

It is possible to trace the 'somewhere' from which the television image came. Walker remembers their early thoughts about a set for a possible segment of film showing a contemporary version of Hades. The film would give the point of view of someone walking down a hotel corridor and looking into a room through a spy hole and a 'figure [Orpheus] would be there watching a television'.[14] This idea was never quite forgotten and almost a year later it emerged, in the changed form of Eurydice's face on the screen of the travelling television set, the central image of a film showing Orpheus' memory of turning around and losing Eurydice.

Figure 11   Dead Wedding: a still image from the animated film representing Orpheus' memory of Eurydice attempting to escape Hades. Photo reproduced by kind permission of Faulty Optic.

From reading Darwin's writings on evolution in *The Origin of Species by Means of Natural Selection* (Darwin, 1985), it can be concluded that it is neither the strongest nor the most intelligent of the species that necessarily survive but those who are most responsive to change. Writers, devisers and other makers of work know that strong ideas do not always survive in the creative pond in which they were spawned. They may become the controlling impetus in another project, but experienced practitioners know when to discard favourite ideas that no longer fit a current scenario, however brilliant they might consider them. The idea/image of the television is an apt example of this type of Darwinian survival as it had the capability to adapt to new circumstances and maintain its integrity and validity in a rapidly evolving scenario; its strength was in its adaptability, not its innate 'rightness', and it re-emerged as a central core of Orpheus' memory.

In the show, the memory is an animated film of a hurdle race from Orpheus' point of view, with him and Eurydice as the competitors. The starting pistol fires, Orpheus sets off around the track, the Eurydice-faced television in hot pursuit. Orpheus breathes heavily as he strides the hurdles, in contrast with Eurydice, whose television-set persona crashes through them, a look of horror on her face. At the finish line Orpheus makes his fatal error, looking back to see where Eurydice is in the race. As the television trundles towards the finish, a nightmarish giant worm-like creature (seen previously in the performance in a film of Orpheus' descent into the underworld) zooms towards her and plunges into the television screen, smashing the image of Eurydice's face. The final part of the memory shows the flaming, smoking, smashed television forlornly retreating to Hades.

In the workshop the running track has been built complete with white lane markings; the television has been made, incorporating a housing and magnifying lens to increase the size of the image that will be played through a small monitor located in the set. A pre-recorded image of Leah Morgan's face is projected from the wee television that is standing on the running track. Glover points a video camera at the television set to record the movement as it is moved up and down the track. This whole image can be seen on another monitor that Walker and I are watching. Morgan makes suggestions and the lighting is changed, along with the size of the image being fed through to the monitor. Everyone is trying to imagine what this will look like when it is projected onto a gauze screen in the performance – the size of the image must be correct as well as its brightness and contrast, as it will be competing with spill from other lighting used in the performance. It is difficult to estimate the lighting needs – at this point in the process it is not clear if the musicians will be visible on stage and if they will need light to read their music (assuming there will be live musicians). Morgan talks about the quality of the video and how it might need to be treated to create the desired effect.

For the first time there is the sense of a team collaborating to find the best way to present the material. With Morgan now a part of the process, the show can no longer remain inscribed in the shorthand that Glover and Walker use to communicate their ideas to each other. Their almost telepathic sense of what is needed from each other is a massive strength when working as a duo, as evidenced by the silent and unseen communication process they use to manipulate a single puppet's movement and action in *Horsehead* and *Soiled*, two shows I have seen them perform. But now they have to articulate these ideas so that Morgan can work with the material to create the desired effect. There is a measure of relief, a welcome letting out of breath as Glover and Walker talk about the video images and ideas with Morgan, and finally are able to play with them in concrete form. This is the beginning of creating performance material, the beginning of the realisation of the ur-play that is inside their heads. After the end of the rehearsal I wonder if the relief that I identified was actually my own rather than that of anyone directly involved with making the show; at last I have been witness to something that I can recognise as the making of performance material.

As the process of making the show accelerates in the autumn of 2006, elements of 'chaos' begin to emerge: the very late identification of Mira Calix as the composer and the sudden emergence of Jim Bond as another collaborator, but one with minimal time to help to imagine, design and build the set. These occurrences require Faulty Optic to adopt an altered sequence to the devising of the performance, forcing them to tackle the fabrication of material, both performance and actual objects, in a counter-intuitive order. This counter-intuitive approach, which asks them to accept the patterns that this 'chaos' provides, forces their process into new directions.

In order to consider the chaotic aspect of this devising process it is useful to very briefly introduce Chaos Theory. It was initially developed by meteorological scientist Edward Lorenz when studying equations to help predict the weather. He introduces the idea that seemingly inconsequential factors at the beginning of a process can have an enormous effect upon the system within which it is operating. This is often expressed in the popular analogy that a butterfly flapping its wings in Singapore can stir up a storm that breaks over New York some time later and, while this is a gross simplification of a small part of Chaos Theory, the analogy is rooted in truth. As Gleick states, the patterns that Lorenz witnessed in his study of weather systems 'signalled pure disorder, since no point or pattern of points ever recurred. Yet it also signalled a new kind of order' (Gleick, 1998, p. 30).

A further look at other systems, such as the growth of insect popu-
lations, showed that they too produced non-repeatable patterns,
non-linear systems, which followed their own logic. Looking at such non-
linear patterns, it was noted that many of these systems operated most
successfully at the edge of chaos, a point in their development when
they were on the edge of complete turbulence but just stable enough
to maintain their own integrity. A good analogy is that of hundreds of
birds taking off from a lake and flying away together. They spontaneously organise themselves into a 'patterned flock' (Sardar and Abrams,
2004, p. 83). It is a feature of chaotic systems that at certain points they
spontaneously self-organise and make novel structures and new modes
of behaviour. In this way they can be described as creative systems, and
it is possible to see this type of pattern in the process of making *Dead
Wedding*. Far from being a linear process that unfolds in a sequential
pattern, it has more affiliation with the non-linear order that Gleick
refers to in his analysis of Lorenz's findings.

The first 'chaotic' element is the extremely small amount of time
available to Jim Bond, the 'mechanical sculptor', who has a sudden gap
in his own busy schedule to come to help design and make the set.[15]
Because of the compressed timescale the company has to make a quick
decision and so determines that a key part of the set will be a stage
area which embodies the shape of a lyre, Orpheus' harp-like musical
instrument. This is a significant decision as it influences the movement
and action of the Orpheus puppet, much of whose performance takes
place upon this area of the set. The lyre-shaped construction also has a
train-like rail-track welded to its top, which allows a small flat-bedded
wheeled cart to move across it. This too will influence much of the
interaction between Orpheus and Eurydice, especially as the Orpheus
puppet has no legs and relies on this cart and some prosthetic legs made
from planks of wood to perambulate around the stage. The set is a major
factor in shaping the performance, rather than merely being a setting in
which action will take place.

The second 'chaotic' element is the late arrival of a musical collaborator, almost eight months into the process. This collaboration with
Calix proves dissimilar from previous ways in which Faulty Optic have
worked with musicians. Rather than sit in on rehearsals and compose
from and around the physical material being witnessed, she will write
independently from written information about the performance action.
The consequence of this is that Glover and Walker must decide upon
quite precise timings for scenes and sequences of action, and also make
clear their emotional temperature. There is nothing implicitly wrong

with this process but at this point in November 2006 they have not yet devised any live performance material. The complexity of Calix's ideas for the music, incorporating cello, viola, clarinets and electronic sound played through her laptop, means that she needs plenty of time to complete the compositional work. Because Glover and Walker are forced to try to guess the timings for scenes and to quickly make decisions about their emotional undercurrents, the action of these scenes will be shaped by the length of the music as much as by other dramaturgical imperatives. This is a creative problem to be solved rather than a headache to be treated, but again is different from the process that the company would usually adopt if they were not working under the particular constraints of this commission. It is the theatrical equivalent of writing poetry to the stricter metric form of a sonnet rather than writing in free verse. Faulty Optic's devising strategies have been forced into different directions by the 'chaotic' elements that are introduced into their creative process.

In December 2006 the animated film part of the performance is growing in complexity to include sections set in Hades and the ghostly figures of the Bacchae, who haunt Orpheus and taunt Eurydice on their wedding day. This wedding section is a mixture of live puppetry and projected film, representing another of Orpheus' memories, leading him to try to recreate the wedding feast to rekindle his and Eurydice's love for each other. These are broad brushstrokes of action at the moment. The puppetry equivalent of basic blocking takes place, and parts of the filmed sections are edited into possible sequences. The fine detail can't be created until all the music, set and puppets are in a state of near completeness. Faulty Optic send Calix a scenario, consisting of all the scenes or sections of action that they think will be in final piece, complete with their timings and emotional temperatures.

In February 2007, five months before the premiere, the workshop space is cold and our breath steams out of our mouths, echoing the hot coffee mugs cupped in our hands. Since New Year, Glover, Walker and Morgan have recorded and edited the animated film sections of the show. In the performance each section of the projected material has a different characteristic, depending upon which part of the dramatic world is being explored. The Bacchae, when appearing in Orpheus' memory, will have an ethereal quality, floating smoothly across the stage. This effect is achieved in the workshop space by experimenting with backlighting gauze onto which the film is projected. The animation that shows dead souls being ferried in coffins across the river Styx has more of a ghoulish, two-dimensional cartoon quality. The film of

Orpheus' recurrent nightmare of his failed attempt to rescue Eurydice uses three-dimensional objects (see Figure 11) and puppets, and most closely resembles the real-time aesthetic reality of the live performance action. Although this footage will be re-edited before the final performance the material now exists in a form that stays constant until opening night. It is one facet of the performance that is now in a relatively fixed state.

In March Glover and Walker decide that they will need a third puppeteer because the action has increased in complexity. Glover steps out of the performance to concentrate on directing the piece, and Morgan is introduced into the performance as a puppeteer. At the next rehearsal, experienced puppeteer Simon Kerrigan appears. As the rehearsal unfolds, it becomes clear that he will be the main Orpheus performer, while Walker concentrates on Eurydice, with Morgan moving between the two. It is worth noting here that the predominant puppets in the performance can be manipulated by one, two or three people; the more people working a puppet the greater the degree of movement and detail that can be achieved. At the most sophisticated level these puppets are manipulated by one puppeteer controlling the head and an arm, another the legs and a third the remaining arm. As I watch the rehearsal unfold it is clear that the puppeteers will need to develop an instinctive knowledge of each other's movements, knowing when to swap hands and able to anticipate each other's actions. In the coming rehearsal period the company will not only need to devise the bulk of the live action but also to develop an ensemble playing style; Walker, Morgan and Kerrigan will need to create and learn the performance language of *Dead Wedding*.

Glover and Walker feed ideas to Kerrigan and Morgan to help them develop the physical action of the scene. The Faulty Optic founders are acting as a mirror, constantly feeding back information about the puppet movement aesthetic that the new puppeteers are striving to achieve. The scale of movement is critically important and they offer fine-tuning advice about the angle of Orpheus' head or the height of a jump. The live action being worked upon is linked with the filmed material on the running track representing Orpheus' nightmare. The animated film plays and Kerrigan synchronises the action of the Orpheus puppet with it: each time a hurdle is reached in the film, the live-action Orpheus puppet also jumps up as if reliving the race. But being in an enclosed space under the lyre-shaped piece of set, each time he jumps he bangs his head on the metal frame above him. The image is both desperately sad and funny as Orpheus tortures himself with the memory of his loss.

But although the image and action work well in this rehearsal, when it comes to rehearsing the show months later the action is discarded: for when performed with full theatre lighting in place, the puppet's action is too distracting from the theatrically subtle narrative of the filmed section. The original action is strong but, unlike the television image, it does not survive and evolve because it is not responsive or adaptable enough to the changed circumstances.

In discussions after this rehearsal, Faulty Optic voice another difference between this process and their previous devising practice. They usually work with the puppets on set to create actions and images that they find interesting, and then find the best way to use this material to create the fabric or associative narrative of the show. But in this collaboration, they have had to fashion a scenario before the practical devising process begins and now have to find images and action that fit with their 'script'. They are being forced to follow the more conventional model of fleshing out a scenario, rather than allowing the narrative to emerge from material exploration. The 'chaotic' process generated by the collaborative imperative has in this instance spontaneously self-organised, making a novel structure (in terms of the usual working practice of this company) and resulting in a new mode of behaviour.

In April Calix delivers drafts of music for particular sections of the performance, and detailed rehearsal begins. Some of the material of the scenes will have to be re-thought as the action that the puppeteers have created will need to be changed to fit the length of the musical score. When they had previously been asked by Calix to establish approximate timings for various sections of the show, Glover and Walker had overestimated the probable length of the scene where Orpheus tries to recreate the wedding feast. Now there is simply far too much music for the length of the action that has been created. The action of the scene must be extended to fit with the score. There is not enough time to recompose the music because of the complex nature of the composition, which involves live instruments working in tandem with electronically produced sound and voice, played from Calix's laptop computer. Time and complexity dictate that action must fit with existing sound.

However, Faulty Optic now knows the parameters of most of the scenes. Over the next week the detailed action is shaped to fit with the music. In a rough run-through, the thematic and poetic links between scenes begin to emerge. At the end of the rehearsal there is discussion about what the performers should wear. The performers will be seen and there will be no attempt to disguise their manipulation of the puppets. The relationship between puppet and puppeteer adds theatricality and meaning rather than spoiling an illusion that the puppets are independent beings. Even in rehearsal this relationship creates a powerful emotional charge, not unlike the thrill of seeing a well-developed physical theatre ensemble working collaboratively onstage, some performers embodying character as others supply physical support.

Pace gathers, and at the end of the second week in May there is a run-through of all the material so that Calix can make some small adjustments to the musical soundscape. Glover mentions that the music is influencing the performance style, making it less 'upfront'. Having not worked together or with the puppets for three weeks, the three puppeteers realise that there is logistical work to be reconsidered: who will animate which puppet head or body or limb at each particular moment? The action has not been fully set or scored, and like dancers supporting each other during physical interactions they must allow their bodies to remember these occurrences. At this moment the show feels crude and awkward because the mechanics of the piece are too visible and the performers have not rehearsed enough to develop the subtlety of performance required. There are many elements that are not realised fully in this run of the show, such as lighting, full integration of sound/music and action, and final decisions on set detail. This results in a chaos of components coming together, making it difficult to see the show as a whole, but Glover must trust that the ideal show that he and Walker have imagined will emerge when all these chaotic elements have been refined and mixed in the right measure.

In June the mixture is almost complete. In Studio 2 at the University of Huddersfield, detail and clarity emerge as the puppeteers and musicians work together, understanding the performance aesthetic. The puppeteers have found the language which allows them to work together to provide detailed action: they are rehearsing a section where Orpheus has collected together many of the belongings that Eurydice has tried to throw away, including their wedding photograph and her wedding dress. He is trying to retain the memory of their happy nuptials, in direct contrast to Eurydice who is doing her best to forget the past and move into her future. Orpheus holds up the tattered wedding dress with one hand and scratches his head with the other. It seems that he can't understand why she won't respond to his attempts to reunite them. The torn dress is a sad symbol of a ruined past that he can't come to terms with and the scratching of his head is an economical and recognisably human indication of his confusion. It might be a cliché in other circumstances but here, in combination with the previous action of Eurydice divesting herself of her belongings and the image of the dress held aloft by Orpheus, it becomes a simple, economical, truthful action that allows an audience to believe in the puppet's dramatic reality and creates an empathetic link between performance and spectator. Improvised by the puppeteers, this and other similarly detailed moments emerge within the broader brushstrokes of larger images and bring a powerful focus to the performance. The show is emerging. It takes a week for Mark Webber, the final collaborator, to provisionally light the piece; lighting is an element integral to the show, providing emotional texture in combination with the soundscape and performance action.

After a final rehearsal with the full cast of three puppeteers and four musicians, everything is in place. Now the show must be dismantled and transported to Manchester for the world premiere on 5 July 2007. And so it opens. Calix's music creaks, scratches, and moves from creating discomfort to moments of spare beauty. Pluto appears playing a giant gravestone-shaped fruit machine. It disgorges pennies when he wins. Orpheus emerges in the gloomy half-light. He has no legs, so scuttles around on crude wooden substitutes or pushes himself on the trolley to move closer to Eurydice, who has emerged from a water-filled drum where she was submerged. She scrubs at her dress, trying to wash away memory, almost ready to make the final journey into the deepest lands of the dead. An animated film shows coffins crossing the river Styx, cadavers with pennies at the ready to pay for their journey. Orpheus re-enacts the wedding feast for Eurydice but has only dusty champagne glasses and dead roses. She rejects him and Orpheus is haunted by memory of his failure to rescue her, her filmed image captured in the television that crashes through hurdles until its screen is smashed by the unnamed giant worm-like creature from Hades. Orpheus is told to let go of her by an enormous head, a representation of his former self. But he takes a hammer to it, beating it into submission. Eurydice sees his distress and holds him one final time. He helps her climb up high so she can jump into the rushing winds to be carried away into peaceful forgetfulness. Orpheus climbs into the water drum. He will now let go of his failure, attempt to find some peace.

As was clear from the enthusiastic audience response to the performance that I saw, many members of the audience, including some reviewers, were enchanted by the show's fractured poetic drive, extraordinary visual and sonic impact and skilful puppetry, along with its 'wonderfully macabre sense of humour'.[16] But some found the lack of narrative arc problematic, one reviewer arguing that the show 'could have shed a little more light on exactly what was going on here'.[17] Glover and Walker decide that for the next performances, at the Huddersfield

Contemporary Music Festival in the Lawrence Batley Theatre, a few more signposts would help to make the performance as accessible as possible to a wide audience, without disturbing its poetic integrity. The order of two middle scenes is changed to provide greater continuity in the story-telling. In consultation with Calix, the positioning of some of the music and sound is altered to provide clearer thematic links between non-sequential scenes. They also decide to add projected text, which appears hand-written in the air. The text is informative and witty, poetically enhancing the narrative of various scenes, opening up the two lovers' relationship, and providing context and irony. She says 'You are my heartstring plucker'[18] and urges him to play his music faster until they both conclude with:

> as one heart
> as one beat
> fast together
> together forever.[19]

In the final performances at the Barbican in January 2008, Glover takes the role of the main Orpheus puppeteer. By now the show has bedded in and has a greater amount of detail in the specific actions of the puppets. Each tiny action has become a character's thought. This detail has been arrived at through the playing of the piece in performance, listening to audience reaction, careful observation and the company's instinctive sense of puppet performance language, built up over 20 years of practical experience. To say that the development of *Dead Wedding* is necessarily complete, though, would be to misrepresent the way in which the company operates. Glover and Walker keep much of their work alive in their repertoire of available shows, and each time these are revisited, changes are made to reflect new developments in their thoughts about the aesthetics of performance, as well as the pragmatics of touring to a wide variety of venues worldwide. For Faulty Optic, as with many companies that keep work in repertoire, the devising process is a continuum, the performances being stopping-off points on the journey of the evolution of the work.

*   *   *

Because Glover and Walker have worked together on all aspects of the production and performance of their work for over 20 years, much of their process is instinctive and organic. Their longevity has resulted in a very strong company aesthetic, which lies not only in the actual fabric of the performance, the puppets, set and use of filmed animated material, but also in the sensibility of the performed material, a unique brand of comic melancholia and often grotesque humour. The strength and innate knowledge of this aesthetic has allowed the company to ride the chaos of making a complex collaborative show over a long period of time. The resulting moments of inertia in the process are not wasted time or unproductive meanderings. They are evolutionary moments when osmosis can take place, the unconscious absorption of the ideas and knowledge related to the performance, allowing the company to make sense of the chaos of the process and letting the performance ideas adapt to new circumstances.

All that I have described in this chapter has been a significant part of the devising process. But the performance also developed in unseen ways outside of the designated performance-making time; in conversations between Glover and Walker in the van on the way to perform *Horsehead*; sharing a meal together; after watching a film. This unconscious work is also a significant part of the way in which these long-term collaborators develop ideas, and helps to explain why they are often uninterested in describing their process and why this description of it is a part but not the whole of the story.

Chronology of productions

My Pig Speaks Latin (1988) Rosemary Branch, London, then national and international tours.

Snuffhouse Dustlouse (1991–4 and 1999–2000) national and international tours.

Darwin's Dead Herring (1993) ICA, London, then national and international tours.

Shot at the Troff (1998) Komedia Theatre, Brighton, then national and international tours.

Bubbly Beds (1998) national and international tours.

Tunnelvision (1998–2000) BAC, London, then national and international tours.

Soiled (2003–4) national and international tours.

Licked (2004) with Edward Carey and Dominic Sales, part of *Resonance*, Leeds Met Studio, commissioned by Opera North and co-produced by Leeds Metropolitan University.

Horsehead (2005–6) national and international tours.

Dead Wedding (2007) with Mira Calix, commissioned by Manchester International Festival, Opera North Projects, and presented in association with the Library Theatre, Manchester. Also played at the Lawrence Batley Theatre, Huddersfield, and as part of the London International Mime Festival and bite08 season at the Barbican, London.

Fish Clay Perspex (2009) Shunt Vaults, London, then national and international tours.

Notes

1. Faulty Optic Theatre of Animation, http://www.faultyoptic.co.uk/ (accessed 2 May 2008).
2. Faulty Optic Theatre of Animation, *Performance Profile*, http://www.britishcouncil.org/arts-performanceinprofile2007-faulty-optic-theatre-of-animation.htm (accessed 29 October 2007).
3. Ibid.
4. Susannah Clapp (2006) 'Critics Review of 2006', http://www.guardian.co.uk/film/2006/dec/24/1 (accessed 19 September 2008).
5. Gavin Glover, conversation with the author at rehearsal, 15 August 2006.
6. Glover and Walker, interview with the author, 17 September 2007.
7. Ibid.
8. Opera North, *Dead Wedding* www.operanorth.co.uk/ontperformanceinfo.aspx?productionid=47 (accessed 29 October 2007).
9. Glover, personal email to the author, 4 July 2006.
10. Glover and Walker (2006) *Orpheus and the Underworld* (scenario).
11. Glover, personal email to the author, 21 July 2006.
12. Glover and Walker, interview with the author, 17 September 2007.
13. Ibid.
14. Ibid.
15. Bond, http://www.jimbond.co.uk/ (accessed 17 July 2008).
16. Kevin Bourke (2007) 'Theatre and Dance Reviews', http://www.manchestereveningnews.co.uk/entertainment/theatre_and_dance/theatre_and_dance_reviews/s/1010/1010689_mif_dead_wedding_library_theatre.html (accessed 19 September 2008).
17. Walker (2007) 'Opera: Dead Wedding, Library Theatre, Manchester', http://www.independent.co.uk/arts-entertainment/music/reviews/opera-dead-wedding-library-theatre-manchester--none-onestar-twostar-threestar-fourstar-fivestar-457382.html (accessed 19 September 2008).
18. Faulty Optic Theatre of Animation, *Dead Wedding* (DVD of Performance 2008, Chapter 5).
19. Ibid.

4
Devising and Advocacy
The Red Room's *Unstated*

Gareth White

> A poetics of human rights is about taking collective responsibility for the performance of rights, and recognising the creative opportunities afforded by envisioning social change.
>
> (Nicholson, 2005, p. 151)

It is a Thursday morning, in a rehearsal studio in North London. Actors sit quietly, some of them attentive, some distracted; a stage manager busies herself; a director and a writer sit thoughtfully. There has been an interruption to the flow of the rehearsal, and a break in the conversation. A woman's face is projected against a white sheet hanging from a wall; in freeze frame, her mood seems to reflect the mood of the people in the room: she looks pensive, concerned but not quite distressed. People here have important things to say, but are waiting until they find the right words to say them.

The actors have been working on a scene created by the writer, Fin Kennedy, based on the words of the woman on the screen. Her name is Victoire (her full name is never given) and she is a refugee who has fled violence and persecution in her home country of Togo. The scene places her – through an actress who repeats some of her words – in an interview room at an Immigration Removal Centre. The actress, Marva Alexander, has just read a speech in which she describes a violent sexual assault, and the murder of her son, as if they were Victoire's experiences. Now Alexander expresses her reservations about using the 'character' in this way, when it is not known if these are really part of Victoire's story. Another actor is concerned about the feelings of Victoire if she should come to see the performance – her son is missing; do the company have the right to speculate about his death?

Kennedy and the director, Topher Campbell, ponder this, and soon agree with the actors' concerns. Kennedy explains a little of what he is trying to do with the scene, and why he has chosen Victoire's story as a medium for these ideas. But he sees that there is a need to be more careful in the way he uses people's testimony. He says 'I'm starting to get the hang of this now,' and sets off to re-write the scene.[1]

This incident takes place early in the rehearsal process for The Red Room's *Unstated*, a piece of devised political theatre that portrays the situation of refugees awaiting admittance into contemporary Britain. The *Unstated* project, and especially this moment, provides an opportunity for reflection on some problems that arise in devised theatre, in political theatre, and in work that uses the testimony of people in vulnerable situations. In this chapter I will outline their devising process, and how its interlocking circles of collaboration (between writer, director, actors, reference group and interviewees) create different kinds of agency in the project. I will conclude with an analysis of how this group of performance makers have made use of other people's words and stories in the best interests of those people themselves. Political theatre which advocates for people – speaking on their behalf rather than involving them directly in the creation and performance of the work – cannot treat its raw material casually, and the processes through which an ethical treatment of this material evolve reward closer attention.

At this point in the process Campbell and some of the actors have been working on this piece, directly or indirectly, for close to two years, while Kennedy – unusually for a writer – has joined the team later. The project began with *Journeys to Work*, a contribution to the @Work Network, a pan-European project in which 'artists, workers, trade unions and policy makers engaged in research, discussion and creative exchange',[2] working on issues of migration into and across Europe. *Unstated* has been developed from *Journeys to Work*, re-using some of the recorded interviews that were the foundation of that piece, but adding more, and developing the live performance substantially.

The issue of asylum is topical, as the Refugee Council, one of the campaigning organisations that are part of the *Unstated* Reference Group, note: 'It is rarely out of the newspapers and is the subject of intense political and public debate. Reporting and commentary about asylum seekers and refugees is often hostile, unbalanced and factually incorrect.'[3] This serves to promote unjustified negative attitudes to refugees, a stigma which is compounded by the inability of people in this situation to speak out to defend themselves, for reasons ranging from language barriers to lack of access to the media, and by the evolving strategy of the authorities to exploit their disadvantages as 'stateless' people. The strategy, according to the Migrants Rights Network, is to treat human rights as earned rather than inherent: that they are granted when a person has been given leave to remain in the country, and can be neglected before then.

This 'rights-free' approach is the target and the motivation for *Unstated,* but it also affects the process through which the piece evolved. At the centre of the work are dozens of hours of interviews with migrants, interviews that were often very difficult to make happen. The authorities at Immigration Removal Centres are not sympathetic to campaigning theatre-makers, and do not allow recording within their walls; migrants who are in the process of making their case to the UK Border Agency or who are trying to avoid deportation can be difficult to track down, often having no fixed address and having plenty of motivation for not telling stories of mistreatment by the British authorities. The performance is aimed at drawing attention to the issue, and to do that because the people who suffer because of it are prevented from speaking for themselves: however the process of creating the work that might speak on their behalf was tricky and troublesome.

Campbell says that 'The Red Room is and always will be a campaigning company,' with a mission to use performance to state the case for left-wing politics, and to defend the most under-represented and vulnerable people in our society.[4] The company's involvement in advocacy for migrants and asylum seekers dates back to its earliest work, including 1996's *Coming to Land* season and the production of Kay Adshead's *The Bogus Woman* in 2000. However, devised work of this kind, which moves eclectically from one form to another, is a relatively new departure for The Red Room. Prior to Campbell's appointment in 2006 their theatre work (they also make films and create, curate and host events of other kinds) mostly consisted of the production of plays in a more conventional sense, often the work of playwrights looking for a forum for political work. Writers such as Anthony Nielson and Adshead have had successes with Red Room productions at key moments in their careers, and these collaborations have won a number of awards. Their writers' group continues to nurture new artists, and to give those who have established reputations a forum to develop work and to experiment. But although the devising that they have undertaken for *Unstated* is a change of strategy, it is connected and continuous with what has come before – Fin Kennedy, for example, has been a member of the writers' group for some time.

They have, since their inception, been explicitly political, which is expressed in their mission statement:

> The Red Room exists to free the imagination against the status quo.
>   We aim to create work that is original, daring, provocative and inspiring, for audiences who question the changing world. We want our work to impact on wider society, so we actively develop our artists and audiences from the widest variety of social and cultural backgrounds. We also involve ourselves in debates and activism around culture and politics. The Red Room believes that theatre should be a genuinely public art form.[5]

Many of these aims are answered in *Unstated* – the piece is provocative and difficult, and presents awkward questions to its audience; it has involved collaborators from communities that are explicitly and deliberately excluded from mainstream cultural intercourse; and it has evolved through a process of engagement on an international level. Following a devised approach on this occasion has also facilitated their attempt to be 'original, daring, provocative', in allowing Campbell and Kennedy to work collaboratively and responsively, and to follow their impulses in a flexible way that a more conventional writer–director relationship can make more difficult.

Though they have such explicit political commitment, this does not extend to the commitment to non-hierarchical working processes which characterised the first wave of political devised theatre described by Heddon and Milling:

> Aligning political ideologies with working practices led many companies to develop collective structures. Rather than one person assuming a position of ultimate control over the theatrical product (the director), and over those who created it (the performers), political companies most often attempted to operate collectively.
>
> (Heddon and Milling, 2006, p. 101)

At The Red Room there is no collective structure, but an enlightened hierarchy: the company is run on a day-to-day basis by Campbell and producer Bryan Savary, with a board to support and supervise the business, specialist part-time and full-time staff, and artists and technicians brought in for specific projects. Campbell's style is essentially autocratic: though he is democratic in his openness to suggestions and his willingness to discuss ideas, there is no ambiguity about who has 'ultimate control'. He regards this as the best way to do political work: to maintain coherence of thought and to be responsive and decisive. In its recognition of a duty to develop audiences and artists, the mission statement shows awareness of the importance of the *process* of theatre-making to its political efficacy, but in the company's theatre work this is realised through the kinds of people and subject that they engage with, rather than a focus on modelling democracy in the process.

An unusual and important element of the process of making *Unstated* was the 'Reference Group' which was set up and met regularly from the initiation of the project, pre-dating the writing and devising of the piece. This group includes representatives of refugee advocacy organisations, the Trades Union Congress and academic researchers. They have contributed in a variety of important ways: for example, connecting the company with the people who have given interviews, providing information and checking facts and interpretations, and marketing the show and connecting it to other campaigns. Though the group's members have not been full partners in the creative process – they have not been asked for or offered direct suggestions for the form or content of the piece – they have influenced the choices that Campbell made about the themes of the work. He says that their most unexpected contribution was to steer the project away from dead-ends and pitfalls, helping the company avoid simplifications and caricatures of the issues. For example, through conversations after *Journeys to Work* and prior to rehearsals for *Unstated*, Don Flynn of Migrants Rights Network suggested that a piece which merely mocked the government's more superficial efforts to address immigration issues – the idea of a 'citizenship test' for example, and its preoccupation with British cultural mores, is a very easy target for comedy – could be a distraction from dealing with more fundamental changes in the rationale for the treatment of migrants.

Although these people and organisations never entered the rehearsal room, they should be recognised as an important part of the devising process. Just as a community theatre company would research the locale in which they are to work (different approaches to which are described in Heddon and Milling, 2006, pp. 130–56), The Red Room committed time and resources to researching the community of interest that is concerned with the issue on which their performance will campaign. Crucially, for a consideration of this as a devising process, this happened before any play was written, and before the writer was brought into the project. It would be possible to look at the whole sequence, from the conception of *Journeys to Work* to the production of *Unstated*, as one process of devising, which would help to explain why the company worked this way on this occasion. Whereas on other projects they have seen their role as championing and realising work initiated by writers, here the commitment to the project and to making a piece about this issue came first, so that it was logical and appropriate for the writers to make their contribution later.

Like *Journeys to Work*, *Unstated* was based on many hours of interviews with activists, asylum seekers, migrant workers and workers in the 'immigration industry'. It was after this research exercise was complete that performers, a writer and a digital artist were brought together in rehearsals to produce a live performance to work with and alongside the video testimony. Another round of interviews was set up, some returning to the people who had contributed to *Journeys* – continuing to follow their story and allowing them to speak in more depth – some with people who had come to The Red Room's attention because of the first show.

Alongside these interviews, while the film crew were together, they shot a range of contextualising and background material – for example outside Harmondsworth Detention Centre, the Houses of Parliament and Lunar House in Croydon, headquarters of the United Kingdom Border Agency (UKBA). These shoots were directed by Campbell, who also directs for television, and in this situation there was a similar organisational structure. The crew knew their roles and made decisions where appropriate, but it was the director's role to choose how to respond to unfolding situations – and with some zealous security guards at these locations, situations unfolded problematically at points. There was a break between the end of the filming and the beginning of rehearsals during which Kennedy and Campbell watched this material and selected what they could use to shape an argument, and began to imagine the performance that could draw the different elements together.

The interviews are shot in different ways, some in settings that are relevant to the story they are telling; for example Afshin Azizian, an Iranian refugee, is seen in his flat, in the park where he taught football to local boys in exchange for English lessons, and in front of an immigration office. Others appear in anonymous rooms and hallways, in a way that seems to speak of the non-places into which the stateless refugee is thrown. Organising and recording the interviews was in itself a long and difficult process – people had conflicting motivations for and against participating. Workers in the industry had concerns about exposure (they may, for example, have signed the Official Secrets Act), and some who had intended to speak of their experiences pulled out at the last minute. Some subjects were also worried that drawing attention to themselves might prejudice their prospects when their cases were heard, and were unable to continue. Liam Byrne, Minister of State for Borders and Immigration, was asked to give an interview but he declined, so instead Kennedy assembled a collage of phrases from several speeches, a bit of licence, and exploited performer Alasdair MacEwen's skills as a mimic. However, once the company had decided to use recorded testimony in the piece, they found that they had made a commitment to people whose words they could not manipulate like this.

Despite his authoritative approach to direction, Campbell did not enter the project with a fixed idea of how the work would develop, and it grew and altered a great deal even after the shooting of the second set of interviews. These changes have partly evolved through his collaboration with Kennedy. Kennedy had been a member of The Red Room's writers' group for four years, but this was his first time as a key writer. He has, in the past, written both entirely independently and in collaboration with groups of performers – sometimes in situations that are closer to the community model of devising. His interest in collaboration and communities is also exhibited in his position as writer in residence at Mulberry School for Girls in Tower Hamlets. He says that working from research or from collaboration are processes that suit him – he has no interest in writing about his own life, and these approaches allow him to access experiences of life beyond his own. His method is to respond to what happens in the rehearsal room and to the research he has seen, read and participated in, a creative process he describes as looking for 'nuggets of originality', around which to build a play. He also sees his job in this kind of work as keeping an eye on the big picture, rationally looking for motifs and images that capture the thesis, but also to 'bring a bit of poetry' to the subject.[6]

Though he says that this project felt a bit like cheating, because he had so much groundwork done for him, he took an active role in the research as well as viewing the material gathered from the interviews. He visited Harmondsworth and Colnbrook detention centres, and spoke to detainees – one of whom contributed a key moment in the show: an incident in which his hand was broken in a struggle with custody officers, and medical care was withheld for some time. On these visits he was not allowed to take even pen and paper into the centre, and had to assemble his notes from memory, bringing them in to the first days of rehearsal to share with the company alongside the taped interviews.

The process of reviewing and selecting footage is where many decisions which shaped the show were made: decisions about how to interweave the stories, and how to find a balance between making a strong case, engaging the audience and indulging in a titillating attention to the misery of others. The decisions about what to put in were tough, as each subject has either a story that deserves to be heard or a useful perspective on the politics of migration. The imperative to make a strong case demands that a way is found to present a lot of information, but also that a lot of information is left out; engaging the audience demands that characters should be given time to develop and engage its sympathies and curiosities, but there are too many people with stories to tell to allow space for all of them to receive this attention. Competing impulses like these had to be negotiated, at the same time as sticking to Campbell's aim to be more austere than they had been in *Journeys*, and not to indulge in sensational dwelling on people's suffering. And these things have to be achieved to a strict timetable: the rhythm of the work was unlike the long, reflective process of most playwriting; once rehearsals were under way Kennedy needed to return to rehearsals regularly with pieces of workable script. This put a different pressure on him as a writer – not an insurmountable one, but one which altered his approach to his work.

Rehearsals began each day with a warm-up, led by Campbell as far as he was able (he was suffering from a back injury throughout the rehearsal period) and shared between other members of the company. When Kennedy was in rehearsal, he took part alongside the actors. Some of the scenes necessitated conventional script work – finding a character's motivation for a scene as it is written, blocking movement, negotiating space shaped according to the design. But here the script was often adjusted on the spot, after brief negotiations with Kennedy, who would provide suggestions and think through the consequences of these changes for the development of the scene.

Some aspects of rehearsal used devices more commonly associated with devised process: for example 'hot-seating' was used to develop characters that were to interact with the audience as they moved around the theatre – this was especially useful in creating the pseudo-professional argot of security workers, for example with references to 'detainees who are what we call "agitated"' and the repetition of the mantra 'for your safety and security'. In these exercises the actors imagined the basis for the behaviour of the workers in relation to the detainees – the conflicting pressures they face from management, the 'clients', campaigners and their own consciences. They also spent some time rehearsing the entrance and the movement of spectators. These audience exercises required anyone not directly involved in the scene who happens to be in the room – director, producer, technical designer, observers like myself – to move repeatedly through the entrance procedure – signing a release form, a bag search, a body search with a metal detector, a photo, a 'retinal scan', and finally the issuing of an ID card. We played awkward customers, pushing the limits of the situation and trying different reactions to the interaction that is invited. The actors practised to find an appropriate balance between witty and authentic ways of responding, and to prepare themselves to keep responding 'in character' over long periods to different kinds of behaviour from audiences. This is improvisation, the classic devising tool, used to develop interludes within a show which is largely scripted.

The four performers of *Unstated* said that rehearsals were, in their words, sometimes grim, often heavy. Knowing the theme itself and the material that would be repeatedly watched and worked with in the rehearsal room, they were not expecting to be laughing in every rehearsal, but some aspects of the working process seemed to make it more difficult for them. Campbell's approach to rehearsals is disciplined and focused, and in this project did not involve much general discussion of the subject matter. Time was spent listening to all the selected interviews, and from that he would lead the exercises that would create the performed sequences to echo and complement them, or they would work on the scenes that Kennedy had written. The performers were not collaborators in the same way that Campbell and Kennedy were, so that effectively the show was devised between the director and the writer, or often by the director alone. At worst this left the actors feeling uninvolved, but at best – an observation that each made independently – the difficulty of the rehearsal period meant that the show itself was difficult for the audience in a very appropriate way, and the performers made it even more unfriendly as the run of performances went on. For Clara Onyemere, Campbell was 'very clever: he set up a rehearsal space that was very tough, quite unsupporting in a way, and quite unforgiving. And through that set up, I think, has come out with a very pure show.'[7]

However Campbell denies that this was a conscious choice, and says that 'the toughness comes from the subject matter.'[8] He describes himself as 'methodological' in his approach, which leads to a level of rigour in his rehearsal room. But, he says, such a small company cannot support a co-operative devising process – when there is only enough money for a four and a half week rehearsal process, the pressures are logistical as well as artistic, 'I am having to make decisions based on my parameters, about what I can achieve, and those are also artistic decisions, and I couldn't piss about for four weeks, so I took the lead very strongly and I'd do it again under the circumstances.' But with eight weeks, he said, he would work differently, taking longer to build a working practice and something approaching an ensemble, and to some degree sharing the decision making.

Southwark Playhouse, the venue for the first run of the show, consists of two adjacent archways under London Bridge Station, and when the trappings of the venue are stripped back it has a stark, institutional atmosphere. This inspired Campbell to transform it into 'Southwark Immigration Removal Centre' and invite the audience to move around it as visitors, rather than to use conventional, differentiated audience and performer spaces. From the moment they arrive at the theatre the audience are surrounded by simulations of the experiences of migrants into Britain: they are searched and issued with identity cards before they are allowed entry. The performers address them as if they are visitors to the detention centre, and usher them from place to place, presenting themselves as a group of not-so-endearingly incompetent detention officers, representatives of 'SWIFT services' – a fictional but convincingly mercenary private corporation to which the 'care' of detainees has been outsourced. The audience are addressed by a cabinet minister, as if they are workers in the newly established UKBA, and told of the good work they are doing in removing undesirables from the country, and of increased targets for deportations in the future.

This is not an immersive simulation of such a centre, however; the tour is interrupted by talking heads, projected onto the walls of the theatre, telling us of the misery of being caught up in the processes of the UKBA. These are the interviews through which the argument of the piece is put forward. Some of them show refugees, some show campaigners and experts. More characters played by the live actors appear and disappear, enacting scenes inside and outside the walls of the 'centre', illustrating different aspects of the argument about the treatment of asylum seekers and continually shifting the focus of the audience to different parts of the two playing spaces and into different relationships with the performances and the projected interviews. In the final scene we see the debate when a middle-class dinner party (complete with cocaine and talk of house price windfalls) is interrupted by the arrival of a badly injured man at their door; will they help this uninvited guest, or turn him away? The performance turns from interactive environment, to multi-media agit-prop, to allegorical realism.

The early parts of the piece, in which they improvise with audience members, presenting themselves as employees at Southwark Immigration Removal Centre, offer the performers considerable freedom. Working on these sections in rehearsal was the time when they had scope to invent characters, and to have fun, joking with each other like co-workers. After the production reached its audience, however, they became tougher with the spectators during these sections – 'Trevor' in particular, a custody officer played by Alasdair MacEwen, who in rehearsals and early performances had a repertoire of workplace banter to make use of, became colder and harder. Marva Alexander's character Janine, too, became less friendly, and she told me that this happened after she got a clearer feeling of what the play was about and what the interactivity is for: 'to throw people into the issue'.[9] It seems that the performers had left behind the need to release their nervous tension during these episodes, and had refocused their energy on making the audience appropriately uncomfortable. The difficulty of the rehearsal process had naturally drained their energy, but getting feedback from the early audiences reminded them of the seriousness that they had wanted to give to the material from the start.

The structure of this devising process, and the emphasis on collaboration between writer and director, did allow the actors to create striking and effective performances without involving them in major creative decisions, but some of them felt that their knowledge and opinions were not put to good use. They acknowledged that having the writer around during rehearsals, which was common to both pieces, and a fairly new experience for all the actors, was a luxury. Being able to ask direct questions about lines as they appeared in the text and about the purpose of each scene allowed them to move further and more quickly with the material. Kennedy had strong opinions about how characters should be played – especially in the later scenes, which were more clearly fictional – but he was flexible and ready to engage in discussion about how they could be interpreted, or even how the scene might be written. Nevertheless the actors' input into the piece as devisers was limited; though at points it was decisive, as I will discuss when I return the rehearsal moment described at the beginning of this chapter.

Another difficulty for the performers was working alongside video, providing a live adjunct to a fixed, recorded text. MacEwen said that he felt detached from the film scenes, that there was 'almost a battle between the film and the live performance', and that this added to the coldness of the experience for him.[10] However video is central to this piece. It might be more accurate to see the live elements as serving to 'warm up' the video, to link them as a continuous event and to connect the audience to them by putting them into a shared context. The words spoken on video overlap with those of the performers: mostly the performers repeat or anticipate the words the interview subjects speak, but at points the live performance elaborates the sense of the video text in different ways. There are sequences of movement that work alongside the video, complementing and contrasting with it rather than reproducing or representing the testimony given on tape. There is, for example, a sequence where three of the four performers move among the audience holding newspapers; they speak fragments of speech that have little meaning, but are evocative, and they fold and tear the paper, using it to mark out precarious territory until they are each standing or sitting on it in a different way. As they move Afshin Azizian appears above them in his different environments and tells his story, and the words of the actors begins to make sense – for example their repetition of the phrase 'ten words of English' has anticipated his account of the ten words taught to him by local boys each time he gave them a football lesson.

The figures that appear in the video are sometimes familiar faces – Helena Kennedy and Natasha Walter, who are known to many from appearances on current affairs television for example – but more often, and more importantly, they are the victims of the UKBA's procedures themselves. It seems that their appearance on screen serves to allow them, and the performance, to speak with authority. Words spoken in performance always have a dubious authority: the habits of theatrical fiction suggest that we should take actors' speeches with at least a pinch of salt. Even in autobiographical work, as Govan, Nicholson and Normington observe, 'there is always a play between what is truthful and what is make believe' (2007, p. 71); even where the performers ostensibly speak of their own experiences truthfully, there is inevitably an element of re-interpretation and re-shaping of experience to make it appropriate or engaging, or a change to the nature of the tale as it is re-told repeatedly. The recorded testimony in this piece makes a claim to a more stable authenticity. It seems to say: 'This is what you are being told by someone who knows, and whose experience cannot be doubted. It has been committed to tape, and will not change under the conditions of performance. Take this as truth.' The rest of the performance complements it, reinforces it and gives it a different immediacy, but is obviously the work of a different kind of theatre artistry.

The testimony spoken by Victoire, which I referred to at the beginning of this chapter, occupies a crucial moment in the piece: it is used to portray the interrogation of a detainee inside 'Southwark IRC', and is the first time the audience are introduced to a refugee, either represented by a performer or through a video projection. However, though her words are poignant and powerful, they are not specific. She mostly describes her emotions about leaving Togo and her treatment in Britain, and only makes vague suggestions of what happened to her in her home country. It is not by chance that Alexander spoke up to express her reservations about how the first draft of the script had made use of Victoire's story and of her as a persona. She and MacEwen had met Victoire during the making of the *Journeys to Work*, and had seen this footage many times as part of that production. They already felt an obligation to her, and a feeling that the testimony she had given, limited as it was, should be treated respectfully (MacEwen commented that the other subjects 'weren't so real' to him at this stage).

Campbell observed later that Alexander's intervention, and her articulation of the problem, were very useful. He felt that they weren't on solid ground with how they were using Victoire's words – the scene they had created was a piece of fiction. Kennedy had wanted to say something specific through the scene which was not apparent in what she had said on tape, and so had taken this approach. He says that this scene was one of the first to be written, and that it was written in a traditional way: 'in isolation, just me and a computer',[11] but that in rehearsal two connected issues arose: the dramaturgical problem of how to create a scene in which the Home Office officials draw out of Victoire the kind of information needed to move the play forward (the company had had no contact with the kind of immigration workers that they wanted to show, so they had no testimony on which to authoritatively base a scene which could show what happens during interrogation); and the ethical problem of the limits to how it is possible to manipulate testimony.

During the discussion at this rehearsal Kennedy considered the problem and contextualised it – he had found in Victoire a vehicle through which to portray some of the horrific experiences that refugees had gone through, but which they had not been willing to speak about on camera. The scene, he had felt, needed more specifics in order to ask moral questions of the audience, to ask them how they felt about the 'culture of disbelief' in which the authorities assume an applicant for asylum to be dishonest, rather than the reverse. The 'culture of disbelief' was central to an important argument that Campbell and Kennedy wanted to make: in particular that it returns in this context precisely because people are not protected from bureaucratic manipulation by a human rights framework, and that this is a step back by at least two decades for the rights of vulnerable people in this country.

Reflecting on his comment that he was 'getting the hang of' the working process, Kennedy says that this was partly about getting used to the relationship with Campbell, and the relationship between his writing and the recorded material, but 'also "getting the hang of" creating a text for performance in the context of having a serious responsibility to real individuals'. When he had based his writing on interviews and primary research with individuals before this, he had fictionalised their stories to protect their anonymity. When he agreed to take the scene away and re-write it, Kennedy's options appeared to be: to add more fiction, perhaps detaching Alexander's persona from Victoire, to reduce the content of the scene to hints about Victoire's past, or to make the scene focus on how her reticence fatally weakens her case to be granted leave to remain as a refugee. He needed to review the tapes to see what detail she gives – much of her testimony is in French, and there was material that has not been integrated into the version cut for the show – and to consider where important ideas like this are given elsewhere. A theme of *Unstated* has returned in a new way in this episode: whereas before the real Victoire had not stated what Kennedy wanted to show in order to shape his argument, now her reticence, as a more subtly fictionalised 'Victoire', fails to state enough to satisfy her interrogators of her own case to stay in the country.

In the final version of this scene, there is far less elaboration of Victoire's experience – it takes place within a metal cage, surrounded by the audience; the two interviewers encourage 'Victoire' to provide a story with details of abuse of some kind, until they seem excited by the merest hint that she has such an experience to offer them. The scene mutates into a slow and exaggerated assault, the dialogue stops and the two interrogators tower over her, tipping her back on her chair, their hands gripping it beside her face, her chest, and between her legs – it is as if their intrusive questioning returns 'Victoire', in her mind, to an actual incident. Then it returns to the semi-naturalistic mode (Kennedy says it has 'a slightly unreal Pinter-esque quality') that the scene had previously been delivered in.

Just what this relationship between testimony and performance amounts to is not immediately clear. It is, I would suggest, invitingly and appropriately ambiguous. There was still disagreement about whether the 'extended, hyperreal' movement in which 'Victoire' is assaulted should have been used, and whether it might suggest actual sexual assaults by Home Office officials – for which there is no evidence. Campbell felt it was necessary, as much to build the dynamics of the piece as to make a point about the interrogation of a traumatised refugee. As elsewhere in the process, the decision about how to proceed rested with Campbell, but in this incident we can see how a company that has not been explicitly structured to devise democratically – as a co-operative, an ensemble or a community – can nevertheless respond ethically together. In this case, those who have gained the insight of a longer engagement with people and situations were able to offer the benefit of their – instinctive – analysis of the relationship between the performance and those it seeks to serve.

Helen Nicholson calls for 'collective responsibility for the performance of rights' (2005, p. 151), a proposition that applies here. The Red Room's very existence is based on a recognition and acceptance of shared responsibility, and in this project they took a creative approach to advocacy for social change, engaging in a performative response to the erosion of human rights. However, within the creative process itself there were ethical obligations that had to be recognised, and though the company was not structured as a collective, these obligations were shared collectively. I do not want to suggest that if Alexander had not spoken up about her misgivings when she did that the production would have been doomed to an exploitative representation of Victoire's experience – it is very likely that Kennedy and Campbell would have worked this problem through themselves independently – but rather that in a devising project in which it had not been considered possible to share responsibility for writing scenes, the responsibility for the ethical content of those scenes was shared across the company anyway, without the need for any explicit agreement that this should be the case. The personal response of the people involved overrode the professional structure.

The nature of this personal response deserves closer examination, in relation to the overall aims of the project. Working with testimony demands that we become witnesses to the lives of others. To be a witness is to recognise an obligation to the person who gives testimony. Dori Laub suggests that there are:

> three separate, distinct levels of witnessing [in relation to traumatic experience]: the level of being a witness to oneself within the experience; *the level of being a witness to the testimonies of others*; and the level of being witness to the process of witnessing itself.
>
> (Felman and Laub, 1992, p. 75; my emphasis)

In the incident that we began with, Kennedy was evolving his relationship as a witness to the testimony of Victoire: he was 'getting the hang of' many things in the process, among them what it meant to be a writer in this situation. All of the members of the company were also discovering how to be a witness; some of them were further along this path at that moment than others, and were compelled to speak from that position and move the work towards a more solid ethical relation to the people whose words gave it a foundation. Devising in an *explicitly* democratic process shares this kind of responsibility around, while those taking part in a hierarchical process might find they have a place to hide from it. But there is no reason to suspect that they will do so. The problem arises, rather, out of the premise of this project: that the company should speak on behalf of the people they wish to support, rather than give them the space to speak for themselves. The company are advocates rather than facilitators. This binary relates to a wider tension between participation and representation, in which contemporary performance of many kinds has rejected representation in favour of a more or less problematised presence. Advocacy in political performance generally chooses representative modes, and this raises the problem of the relationship between the work and those it represents; but this is a reason for informed reflection rather than the rejection of advocacy per se.

Advocacy in the sense that it is used in British legal systems is a position of power – a place from which to represent the case for another, to present their best case on their behalf. Why should we do this? Because these others are unable to, or because we are better placed to, or because we feel an imperative not to be silent about their case. Advocacy, in this sense, demands confidence that we speak well, that we speak accurately and that our speech can make a difference. Speaking well, in theatrical terms, is about trust in our abilities and those of our collaborators. Knowing that we make a difference is about faith in our art form, and about realistic understanding of its reach. This is tricky, contingent stuff: theatre-making always risks failure. Speaking accurately might seem a matter of more reliable judgement, but its toes are trodden on by the other two – can we be entirely accurate and speak eloquently? Can we speak strongly enough to make a difference while being entirely accurate? These pressures upon the imperative to speak accurately are at work in the making of *Unstated*.

There is another, contrasting, idea of advocacy: citizen advocacy, as described in Race (2003) for example, insists on the befriending of the other, rather than speaking for them. To put it simply: a person recognised and respected in the community associates themselves with one who is unvalued, and through this association that person becomes visible, and gains value in the eyes of those who did not see it in them before. Their rights are supported through increased access to informal support networks, rather than through the actions of others. The effects of citizen advocacy are partly performative – it makes the under-valued other visible, giving them a place in the performance of everyday life. The participatory practice of applied theatre often takes this tack: it seeks to make a person visible in a valued cultural sphere.

In the community of The Red Room it seems that Victoire had become, briefly, an object: her video testimony available to be manipulated, although in the interests of the piece and by extension in her own interests. For Alexander, Onyemere and MacEwen, she returned as a subject with independent interests of her own. It was their previous association with her that prompted them to adjust their behaviour in an informal way during rehearsals; they had in effect become citizen advocates (informal allies without a position of authority), for her during the devising of *Unstated*.

Chronology of selected productions

The Censor (1997) directed by Antony Nielson, Finborough Theatre and Duke of York's Theatre.
The Bogus Woman (2000) directed by Lisa Goldman, Traverse Theatre.
Animal (2003) directed by Lisa Goldman, Soho Theatre.
Hoxton Story (2005) directed by Lisa Goldman, Hoxton Hall and environs.
Journeys to Work (2007) directed by Topher Campbell, Copenhagen Festival.
Unstated (2008) directed by Topher Campbell, Southwark Playhouse.

Notes

1. Fin Kennedy, email to the author, 29 July 2008.
2. 'About The Red Room', *The Red Room*, http://www.theredroom.org.uk/about. htm (accessed 11 July 2008).
3. 'Press Myths', *Refugee Council Online*, http://www.refugeecouncil.org.uk/ gettinginvolved/campaign/campaigners_pack/press_myths.htm (accessed 31 July 2008).
4. Topher Campbell, interview with the author, 22 July 2007.
5. *The Red Room* website, op. cit.
6. Kennedy, email to the author, 29 July 2008.
7. Clara Onyemere, interview with the author, 12 July 2008.
8. Campbell, interview with the author, 22 July 2007.
9. Marva Alexander, interview with the author, 12 July 2008.
10. Alasdair MacEwen, interview with the author, 12 July 2008.
11. Kennedy, email to the author, 29 July 2008.

5

The Distance Covered

Third Angel's *9 Billion Miles from Home*

Philip Stanier

Alex Kelly and Rachael Walton established Third Angel in Sheffield in 1995 and remain its joint artistic directors, devising, directing, designing and performing in the works made, alongside a range of regular collaborators. Third Angel, however, cannot be simply defined as a theatre company, as its work includes performance, theatre, live art, installation, film, video art, documentary, photography and design. The 40 or more distinct projects that Third Angel has made since 1995 have taken a variety of forms, usually favouring an experimental approach to the creation and presentation of the work. While much of this output has been shown in theatres across the UK and Europe, the company's work has also been sited in 'galleries, cinemas, office blocks, car parks, swimming baths, on the internet and TV, in school halls, a damp cellar in Leicester and a public toilet in Bristol'.[1] I followed the development of one of these projects, *9 Billion Miles from Home*, from early in 2006 to its performance in a finished form late in 2007.

Journeys real and fictional

Third Angel actually began working on *9 Billion Miles from Home* in 2005, its overall genesis taking nearly three years. What distinguished the making of the piece, and what will form the central subject of this chapter, was the distance it covered through the numerous performance events it produced while in development. In fact, the process of making *9 Billion Miles from Home* resulted in a total of six separate performances consisting of three radically different works-in-progress, an after-dinner intervention, a balloon launch and the final performance itself. So the question of distance is crucial as the piece, which is a response to the *Voyager 2* spacecraft and thematically about ideas of distance and solitude, came a long way from where it set off.

Another area of interest in this study is Third Angel's use of both factual and fictional material, a typical strategy for a company that is 'used to making work that strays into the grey area between truth and fiction, memory and imagination ... work that incorporates documentary detail and fiction but doesn't bother to point out which is which' (Kelly, 2000, p. 49). In this project, the 'documentary detail' included both information concerning the *Voyager 2* spacecraft and Kelly and Walton's biographical material. Walton is careful to point out that although most of the company's work 'has elements of autobiography (and biography) in it, as we often draw on our own experiences in making the work' it is not 'confessional theatre'.[2] Again, there is ambiguity as to what is 'true' to a particular performer and what is not, as, Walton continues, 'often a performer can end up telling a story that comes from someone else. We mix elements of fact and fiction all the time.'

What makes *9 Billion Miles from Home* so interesting is that each of the different incarnations of the performance used a different tactic for dealing with the same factual material on the *Voyager* spacecraft and in using autobiographical material, in a way that meant that each new approach to the material further developed the overall project. Third Angel's methodology for this project, then, was to take the initial idea and repeatedly develop and test the material it produced through a series of opportunistic and scheduled performance events.

The performance of information

> Initially, ideas for projects spring from stuff we're interested in. Stuff that bothers us. The news. Things going on in our own lives, and our friends' lives. Some might be sparked off by seeing other work or reading – fiction and non-fiction – or seeing something on TV. We might have an image (found or drawn ourselves) in a sketch book.
>
> (Kelly, 2000, p. 49)

The idea for *9 Billion Miles from Home* initially stemmed from Kelly's interest in the *Voyager 2* spacecraft and its relation to human experiences of time and distance. It began at an event called 'Three Minute Warning' in Bristol in March 2005 (where artists were invited to perform three-minute pieces) and then reappeared at a scratch event (a work-in-progress showing) in Edinburgh in September 2005. At this point the piece took the form of a lecture-demonstration, with Kelly simply reading a passage of text from the 'Golden Record' (a recorded collection of greetings, images and music stored on the *Voyager 2* spacecraft as a message to any extra-terrestrial life forms that might encounter it) and then performing an on-the-spot spoken visualisation of the journey that he would need to take in order to travel from the site of the performance to the location of his birth. Kelly's concern in this performance was in the way the *Voyager* text and the personal material interrelated. In the after-show discussion for the piece, Kelly asked the audience if they felt that there was a connection between the two texts. An audience member responded that the *Voyager* text made Kelly's journey 'sound epic'. The effect of the documentary information on the personal would remain a core theme of the project throughout its development.

I first encountered what became *9 Billion Miles from Home* at a scratch night in Leeds in 2006. By this point the performance had become a duet with Walton, and included information on the *Voyager 2* spacecraft (including a scaled demonstration of *Voyager's* distance from earth using a melon and peppercorns), more material from the record (including text, physical depictions of the images of humans within it and a description of a Pulsar map), the use of walkie-talkies to communicate outside the performance space and the exploration of personal journeys. Like its previous incarnation, the piece was searching for a way to articulate a personal connection to the journeys of the *Voyager* spacecraft. The clash between the personal responses to experiences

Figure 12 A moment from the final version of *9 Billion Miles from Home*. Photo by Christopher Hall.

of distance and travelling, and the fascinating but also inconceivable facts about *Voyager*'s distance from us, which remained unresolved in this performance, would sit at the heart of the devising sessions I was subsequently to attend.

The next rehearsal took place over a weekend in the summer of 2006 at Prema Arts Centre in the village of Uley in preparation for a work-in-progress performance that had been scheduled at the Chelsea Theatre, London, as part of its annual *Sacred* season of live art. On a superficial level, not much seemed to happen during this rehearsal period in terms of developing content or an outline for the forthcoming show. There was a great deal of discussion about the project and its subject matter, and experimentation with small moments of performance, but the main practical activity was the production of a series of small globes which were hung in the space to represent planets or stars. Other activities included:

- An audit – Kelly and Walton shared all of the material created and gathered so far; books on *Voyager 2* and outer space, websites of interest, ideas and stories.
- A list of everything done to date – Where all the activities and actions already done are put down on paper.
- The 'What is this show about' task – The company listed all the possible themes and ideas that the show could examine, and then compared lists and discussed them, removing items as they went and shortening the list to reach a more precise agreement of what the show was about.
- Working with objects – Making, setting fire to, piercing and spilling the contents of the globes.
- Performing material alongside the globes – Placing images or actions gathered from research or earlier performances together in the space.

These activities are typical of Third Angel's methodology, which Kelly describes as featuring:

> lists of ideas on big sheets of paper, some sort of set or defined space to work in (might be a stack of 20 filing cabinets, might simply be a table and two chairs), piles of research material (books, magazine and newspaper articles, printouts from the internet), a video camera and TV monitor [and entailing] discussion, improvisation, argument, research, writing, drawing, video watching ... some rule based devising

exercises and games to get us going … a bit of text or a task or an idea for an image or piece of action that we will try out.

(Kelly, 2000, p. 49)

Kelly's analysis of the various ways in which 'ideas' develop from such activities is interesting in that it includes both deliberate and rational problem-solving – 'concentrated analysis of a problem or effect we want to achieve' – and the unpredictable emergence of ideas or solutions out of accident, boredom or exhaustion:

Sometimes a great idea or piece of material doesn't come until we're getting bored and frustrated with an exercise because we've been doing it so long that we're knackered. Sometimes great ideas come along when we're just having a laugh in the rehearsal space, playing with a new toy.

(Kelly, 2000, p. 49)

What occurred over that devising period was what Kelly and Rachael later termed 'trying the material'. When asked to clarify what this meant, they itemised the following methods of working with material:

- trying material to get started
- trying material to generate further material and for discussion
- trying material at the same time or sequentially for comparison
- trying material to decide on its final inclusion in the performance
- trying material with an audience to gauge their response.

Yet, while most of these methods were employed in the rehearsals I observed, it was clear that a concrete show was not being constructed. There was no discussion of what a beginning or end might be, nor of how the material might fit together, nor of how it might be performed. However, the apparent lack of progress belied an intense honing and agreement over the central concerns of the performance.

This apparently secondary, but actually essential, activity occurred alongside the experimentation with the globes. In retrospect, this strategy of not defining the final show was crucial to the development of the project. There was a genuine sense of relaxation and absence of pressure during the process. Rather than generating a surplus of perhaps irrelevant material, Kelly and Walton spent the time on developing their understanding of how they each related to the material. Without this, the piece would not have been able to make the progress it was about to.

Walton has since noted that the weekend was a shift in their response to the factual content of the piece, 'the start of a departure from an obsession with *Voyager*, away from science, towards [the question of] why *Voyager* was so interesting'. With this came the realisation that the piece was 'about solitude' and that this discovery would require them to 'make a big leap'.[3]

A dinner party

A brief intervention occurred shortly before the showing at Chelsea Theatre. I was hosting a group of performance reviewers who were participating in a training workshop. Part of their training would involve them attending an evening meal at which a guest artist would make a conversational performance intervention, which the reviewers would then be asked to critique. Kelly ended up being this artist. His intervention began as an after-dinner conversation with me, in which he spoke about travel and distance, and then about a series of postcards that he had received as a child from his father in America. He then produced these postcards from his pockets, one by one, read each one aloud and put them on display in the centre of the room. With each of these, he also handed out another postcard bearing information about the timeline of the *Voyager* spacecraft, which we were invited to send to ourselves in the mail. The performance, then, slipped from the conversational, the 'real', into the theatrical, while never constructing a fiction, or returning to the form of a lecture-demonstration that had been used in the early stages of the project. While the central issue of the earlier works-in-progress was a fascination with information, this was not the case in this presentation. Nor was it concerned with fictionalised narratives. Instead the method and primary concern of the piece was a theatricalised engagement with actual experience.

What Kelly had done was to merge one existing project, *23 Postcards from America*, with the timeline of *Voyager*. His realisation of the compatibility between these two areas of interest was an example of what is described on the Third Angel website as 'serendipity in the devising process' and their 'trust in chance and coincidence'.[4] In the same way, a project that was not intended to be part of the devising process for *9 Billion Miles from Home* turned out to be exactly that. The presentation 'clarified that the piece was about communication between humans, and [that] *Voyager* isn't a message to an alien race but a letter back to the human race from the human race'.[5] *9 Billion Miles from Home*, in a peculiar fashion, was partially devised through a dinner party.

Third Angel's exploitation of such one-off performances as part of the devising process is an extension of the way in which many devising companies blur the distinction between process and performance, for example in work-in-progress showings. For Third Angel, a series of 'scratch' nights and side projects formed part of the rehearsal process.

Even though each of the incarnations described so far was considered as a discrete event, they were also rarely 'finished' pieces in their own right, but rather either mutations of existing works or works-in-progress. This allowed greater risks to be taken in terms of the form and structure of each performance, and much more artistic ground to be covered in terms of content.

An unworkable space

Observing the rehearsals in Uley led me to expect that the work-in-progress showing at the Chelsea Theatre in October 2006 would take the form of a lecture-demonstration with additional visual material, perhaps with more personal content. Instead it was a very different piece altogether. Third Angel had produced a performance environment in which isolated fragments served to explore notions of distance, survival and solitude. The performance space was filled with a host of small white globes hanging from the ceiling. As the performance began each one was slowly lit while a recorded voice read out a series of zeros and ones (a binary code sequence locating the position of earth taken from the Pulsar map included on the *Voyager 2* spacecraft). This voice-over of ones and zeros continued throughout the entire performance.

Walton and Kelly entered the space together but throughout the performance they each undertook a series of actions in seeming isolation. For example, Walton let out a long painful scream, to which Kelly did not respond; Kelly used a manual tin opener to pierce a hole in one of the tins he had taken from a collection strapped around his chest, and drank from its contents. Despite the noise and effort of this action Walton did not acknowledge Kelly's presence. It was if they were each alone in the space. This isolation continued throughout the performance, particularly in a sequence where Walton spoke into a walkie-talkie that she had produced from a bag, trying to see if anyone would respond – no reply. The only moment when some sort of exchange was suggested was when Walton asked a series of questions about how far away someone was from certain places or experiences (from running water, from the tallest building they had ever climbed, a hospital, a cloudy day, being happy). Kelly attempted to answer these (describing physical distance or an amount of time past or yet to come) but in a way that did not acknowledge the questioner.

The pattern set up by these spoken monologues was broken when Kelly and Walton walked amongst the globes hanging in the space and, by pulling loose strips of tape beneath each globe, allowed a stream of rice contained within the globe to spill out onto the floor. Each stream produced a neat circular heap on the floor. Walton made a variety of patterns and scatterings in the heaps of rice with her bare feet while Kelly described a journey from the venue to the place he was born. The piece closed with a return to the pattern of isolated speech: Walton sat on the floor and described herself into her walkie-talkie (listing aspects of her physical appearance, people she had met, fights she had been in and places she had travelled to, though without ever recounting any of these stories). Finally Kelly described an image from the *Voyager 2* spacecraft, a diagram of a man and pregnant woman outlined by a perfect circle. The lights dimmed and the show ended, the ones and zeros still counting.

Kelly and Walton had stated in the rehearsals that they felt that they could take risks at the performance, pushing the practice in a direction they had not gone before. Risk is an important tenet of Third Angel's devising methodology and one that was critical to the creation of *9 Billion Miles from Home*. It often means their radically altering a fundamental element of the performance without being certain of the kind of performance they would eventually produce, or of how an audience might respond to it. In the Chelsea Theatre showing they did this by removing much of the content that explained what the show was conceptually about, substituting this explanatory material with material that dealt with their emotional response to the subject matter. The point had become to 'make a work inspired by *Voyager*, but not about it'.[6] In this respect, the performance was very different from their recent work.

That said, in many ways this production also represented a return to earlier ways of working, 'going back to some of the really early work, which has a fictional world but is still not a play. So you take your audience into a world, where they put things together.'[7] Walton indicated that the company had two specific productions in mind throughout the creation of *9 Billion Miles from Home: Saved* (1998), a performance installation about the slow disappearance of a character called Sandra, and Impact Theatre's seminal production *The Carrier Frequency* (1984). Both of these pieces involved the creation of a highly realised fictional space, as well as the fragmented layering of spoken text. In each case, the creative methodology was to create a built environment, and then explore its ability to address the themes specific to each project.

This return to earlier approaches to working, both their own and that of another company, is indicative of Third Angel's willingness to experiment not only with content and form, but with creative process. They regard the development of their own creative methodology not as a linear progression, but as a 'multi-stranded' practice, in which 'strands connect and sometimes we go back along a strand to the last junction and go off.'[8]

The piece was both difficult and engaging, and the after-show discussion divided the audience: those that had seen earlier versions of the project liked it, while those that had not were not quite sure how to engage with the piece. Kelly and Walton themselves were not satisfied with the piece as it stood. As they diagnosed it, the problem lay with the relationship between the fictional spaces pertaining to each performer (and, indeed, the audience): Kelly, Walton and the audience were each in their own ambiguous but clearly separate 'world'. The performance, then, was only being held together by the onstage environment. Ultimately they had created an unworkable space where the different actions and fictions created within the piece failed to work alongside each other. This stage of the process, then, identified a core issue that would need to be resolved in the next major stage of development: the reconciliation of the space, the individual performances and the audience with the material that inspired the performance. But tackling this issue would have to wait until after a balloon launch.

A balloon launch

It was at this stage that a further opportunity arose for the company to make a new piece of work on the theme of distance, in a piece entitled *The Expected Lifespan of Dreams* (2006). The project, part of a Sheffield-based event called *Light Night*, would also allow them to explore their long-running fascination with a Norwegian town which lays claim to a very peculiar characteristic. Due to meteorological anti-cyclone tendencies, this particular town receives the highest number of fallen balloons launched in Europe. Also, this is a town which people suffering from seasonal affective disorder and depression are recommended to visit, due to the positive health-giving effects of its altitude and the quality of its air and light. Kelly and Walton decided to explore this phenomenon through a balloon launch in which participants would be invited to send balloons and positive messages for the inhabitants of the town, and Third Angel would test how many of these would reach the town. So, on *Light Night*, in the Site Gallery café, eight members of the public at a time were presented with information on the town and invited to write 'a hope for the future', as the company put it, attach it to a balloon and launch it in hope of its future arrival in Norway.

There are two aspects of the project that are relevant to the themes of *9 Billion Miles* and that mark it as a stage in its development. First, it is a continuation of the themes of distance and of messages sent over great distances – the messages of hope might remind us of the *Voyager* messages to extra-terrestrial species and perhaps also of Walton's seemingly one-sided walkie-talkie transmissions. Second, there is the fact that all the information concerning the town is entirely fictional. The company's tendency not to disclose the truth or falsehood of apparently factual information is clearly demonstrated here. Again the company had shifted its approach. Rather than ask the audience to absorb actual information, or suspend disbelief, or move from the factual into the fictional, *The Expected Lifespan of Dreams* functions as a generous hoax. One in which the audience become complicit in supporting a bizarre pseudo-scientific experiment and invest emotionally in a fiction which is staged as truth. It is generous, as the aim of the piece is not to 'get one over' on its audience. The company, working with collaborator Chris Thorpe, constructed fake evidence, but left out what they thought would be the most convincing and absurd evidence. In effect the piece gave you enough proof to want to believe but to doubt yourself at the same time. Crucially, audience members invested in the fiction and launched their balloons, taking the event with them out into Sheffield and making the event to some extent 'real'.

In one respect, the project had no immediate bearing on *9 Billion Miles from Home* and its final form. Yet at the same time the performance marks the move to working with distance through performative events and rituals, which was to become the final form of the show.

Balloon debate

Another significant change occurred at this point: Walton stood out of the project to become an 'outside eye' and another collaborator and performer, Gillian Lees, was brought in. Kelly and Walton felt that Lees' familiarity with Third Angel's work, together with her own task-based approach to devising, would help take the piece where it needed to go in the three-week rehearsal period they had before the final performance, again scheduled at the Chelsea Theatre. Indeed, after being brought up to speed with the project so far (which took several days), Lees was quickly able to suggest a new direction. Kelly described a significant moment in the rehearsal:

> There had been a discussion in the first week about a circle in a rectangle, establishing two worlds, the task-based performer world of the stage – the rectangle and the circle being the *Voyager* record, a more fictional space. Then during that first week the question arose of how do you make a perfect circle of talcum powder? Gillian said 'if it's hard to do, you do it in front of audience, and if that is the show, making circles, what ways of doing that are there?'[9]

So in the first week of devising with Lees, a structural principle for the show was identified and a series of tasks had been suggested. Kelly's entry in his notebook at the end of the first week defines the developing performance as a 'ritual':

> Time, distance, circles. ... A ritual for two people, either person could take either role. ... A ritual that is half-set, half-scripted. Half-free response – genuine response on the day, put the audience on both sides – make them more like witnesses. A cyclical ritual – we can see that it has happened before.[10]

To all intents and purposes this was a basic description of the finished show I was to see a short time later in London. Yet although they had hit on the core principle of the performance in the space of just four days, it would take them longer to recognise that this is what they had done. A week later the key components of the show had been created, and yet they were still working with old material and other exercises. Walton notes that 'the description [in the notepad] betrays what was still there.'[11] For the company, there was still so much material from the project's previous incarnations, that they had not realised they had proposed their own solution to the problems of the piece. As Walton commented, 'we were making the show we have now, but it was buried under all the material we still had.'[12]

In the second week, two things acted as catalysts to the project. The company watched a recording of the performance *Journey to the Lower*

World (2004) by artist Marcus Coates, in which Coates performs a shamanic ritual for the residents of a tower block scheduled for demolition. This led them to consider the notion of a shamanic journey and how a ritual format might be employed for the performance. They also conducted research into the Clock of the Long Now, a US-based private scientific project to make a clock that can last for 10,000 years. This gave them the notions of the 'big here' and a 'long now', which are central to the piece. As the company latched onto the idea of the shamanic journey and of these notions of alternative forms of time and space, they were able to focus on the core of their piece, quickly dropping extraneous material. Thus, the process of that final devising period was not unlike a balloon debate, with the company testing and ejecting the non-essential material they had produced, until they arrived at a form that reconciled the material, their performances and the work's relationship with the audience.

9 Billion Miles from Home

The final incarnation of *9 Billion Miles from Home*, at the Chelsea Theatre in 2007, was a highly refined ritual performance. The separation between the fictional and factual and theatrical and actual had been resolved

Figure 13   Talcum powder circles from the final performance of *9 Billion Miles from Home*. Photo by Alex Kelly.

through the process in a way that meant that the imaginary and theatrical material brought us closer to some kind of reality, rather than further away. The isolated fictional spaces that had separated Kelly and Walton in the work-in-progress showing were now reconciled with each other and with the built environment they had created in the venue. This was most obvious in the mechanism that literally joined Kelly and Lees together and to the space: climbing harnesses around their waists were attached to a single rope which ran from the back of one harness to the wall, over the lighting rig, and down the opposite wall to the second performer's harness. The rope was kept taut throughout the performance, each performer leaning forward to give only just enough rope for the other performer to fulfil a series of circle-drawing and other tasks, and no more. As one performer moved into the space, the other had to back away.

The opening task, enacted simultaneously by each performer, echoes the rice circles that had poured out of the hanging globes in the work-in-progress presentation. With a squeeze of a hand, and a metallic double click, soft white powder fell from a silver cylinder to the floor. For a moment the performer operating the dispenser considered where the powder had fallen, and then moved slightly before dispensing some more. Slowly and patiently, click by click and one small cloud of white powder after another, the performer worked to complete a luminous and perfectly formed circle on the pitch-black floor. It was clear that the task had began before the audience entered and the symmetry of the space and activity, the slow pace of action and the simplicity of the white circle lent the performance a quiet meditative atmosphere that drew the audience in, even before the performance had even officially begun. The audience, on two banks of seating facing each other across the performance space, which was lit by two single lights in opposite corners, were very close and palpably silent.

Later circle-drawing tasks included sketching a chalk circle on the nearest wall of the space using a sudden circular swing of the straight arm. Kelly's surprising dexterity in doing this produced spontaneous applause from the audience. Kelly drew another circle, this time with his toes in the powder on the floor as the lights dimmed in expectation of something occurring. These actions were later also performed by Lees – the performance repeated itself half way through, with Kelly and Lees swapping roles in each section.

A joint introduction to the audience followed the first circle-drawing task, marking the formal beginning of the show and making explicit the form that the performance would take and the ideas it would explore:

> We're going on a journey, we're performing a ritual, we want to live in a big here, we want to live in a long now, we want to let things take as long as they take, and we're coming to understand that we can't do it on our own.

Thus, the expositional material that had been removed from the first work-in-progress made a return, but in a brief and somewhat abstracted form that provided the audience with a means of engaging with what was to come, without the need for further exposition. The faint mysticism of this introductory statement was undercut when Lees listed all the components that would be needed to make the performance happen, including a rope, two harnesses, a woman, a man, unscented white talcum powder and so on until concluding with the audience being identified as witnesses. This act of listing made the audience aware of their complicity and partial ownership of the event, and increased our investment in its success.

The *Voyager* spacecraft, which had first inspired the performance, found its place in a sequence in which Lees and Kelly adopted the image of Man and Woman from the *Voyager 2* spacecraft while simultaneously analysing its symbolism. For example, Kelly discussed how the gesture of the raised right hand is a not a sign of dominance, but one of greeting. When this sequence was repeated, it was Lees who raised her hand and spoke, a reversal that undid the apparent gender imbalance posed by the earlier presentation of the image.

The notion of the shamanic journey, inspired by Coates' work, was evoked in two mirrored sections. In the first Kelly moved to the centre of the circle and stood still in the space, his eyes closed, apparently focused on a mental activity that we could not understand from the outside. The sound of a muffled drumbeat, like an amplified heartbeat, found its way into the space; it grew louder and was soon joined by the sound of laboured breathing. The sound began to dominate the space and developed more aggressive and oppressive mechanical textures until its abrupt ending broke the spell. Backing out of the circle as if he was recovering from some internal effort, Kelly described a mental journey he had just taken into the 'big here', a sort of out-of-body experience in which he followed a trail of light connecting his body to all the places he had ever visited in his life, then beyond the Moon until he reached the *Voyager 1* spacecraft at the farthest edge of the solar system, at which point he travelled back to earth and to the performance space. The performance balances in this moment the intimate scale of the Earth-bound, personal journeys that one might take in the course of one's life against the epic scale of the *Voyager* project.

Lees' equivalent moment was marked by the same position in the centre of the powder circle and the same intense soundtrack, but her journey took a different form. For the duration of the noise, she ran on the spot, pulling against the rope that was held taut by Kelly. When the noise ended, to the audience's surprise and despite her obvious exertion, Lees continued her running on the spot while attempting to answer a series of questions posed by Kelly about how far she was in time from certain personally important locations or experiences. In each of these shamanic moments, Kelly's 'big here' and Lees' 'long now', we see a return to the use of autobiographical material.

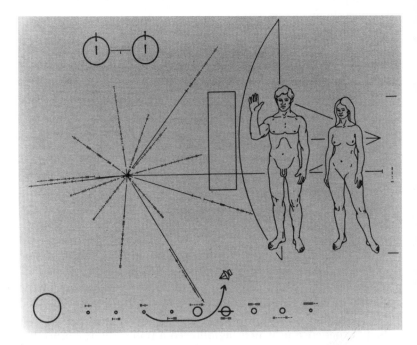

Figure 14 The Voyager plaque – the performance reproduces and interrogates these gestures of greeting. Photo by NASA.

The performance concluded with Kelly and Lees sitting beneath the lights to share the following speech:

> There is a room, and there are witnesses, a rope. There is a woman, she chews her food thoroughly, likes to laugh. There is a man, he is of a happy disposition, has trouble sleeping. The man has been on a journey. The woman has been on a journey. He thinks he can see a bigger here. She thinks see can see a slightly longer now.

The audience were left in quiet contemplation. For me, the effect of the performance was a profound recognition, a sense of seeing my own life reflected in the spatial and temporal journeys of Kelly and Lees both within the small immediate and intimate time and space of the performance, and within the inconceivably immense scale of space and the vast stretches of time that flow through it.

The distance covered

The crucial factors in making *9 Billion Miles from Home* the unique project that it became were the identification of a fruitful point of investigation, and the serendipity that afforded the company a series of contexts to show their work. Without the work-in-progress showings, the dinner party and the balloon launch, Third Angel might have only produced a single performance. Instead the company produced a lecture-demonstration, autobiographical monologue, environmental collage, the hosting of a fake research event/balloon launch and a performance ritual. Moreover, the final performance would not have taken the form it did without the 'multi-stranded' but parallel and back-tracking set of paths that these projects enabled.

Formal experimentation in response to chosen subject matter is a strategy typical of devising practitioners, who will often develop and change their creative approach with each project. What this account of Third Angel's *9 Billion Miles from Home* demonstrates is the extent to which opportune public performances, 'side projects', can become integral to the development of the work. In particular, it illustrates how such events can allow a company to take creative risks. Projects like this allow a company to apply or shape their practice to fit new contexts, and to generate unexpected coincidences and discoveries in terms of subject matter and creative strategy, which go beyond the day-to-day activity of the rehearsal room. The principles of interrogating and exhausting all ideas and contexts, of taking risks, of giving work time to develop and of attempting to cover as much distance as possible are those required to enable the potential of performance to flourish.

Chronology of selected productions

2007

9 Billion Miles from Home, Chelsea Theatre, London.
Listen Up, Totley Infant School, Sheffield.
Curso De Encenação De Teatro, Fundação Calouste Gulbenkian, Lisboa.
Compendium, House 14, Leeds Metropolitan University.
Off The White, Hospital Miguel Bombarda/Culturgest, Lisboa.

2006

32 Conversations About Everyday Life, University of Hull @ Scarborough.
Presumption, Sheffield Theatres Studio.
The Expected Lifespan of Dreams, Site Gallery, Sheffield.

2005

The Lad Lit Project, Sheffield Theatres Studio.
All 2 Gether Now, various locations in Harehills and Burmantofts, Leeds.
Palm, home, London.
Standing Alone, Standing Together, Millennium Gallery, Sheffield.
Clipboards, http://www.thirdangel.co.uk/archive.php?id=35, Sheffield Theatres Studio.

2004

Realtime, Wonderful, Visions of the Near future, hosted by Arnolfini, Bristol.
Hurrysickness, Wickham Theatre, promoted by Arnolfini.
Curso De Encenação De Teatro, Fundação Calouste Gulbenkian, Lisboa.
Pleasant Land (installation and performance), Leeds Met gallery.

2003

Pleasant Land, http://www.pleasantland.org.
Stage an Execution, Nationaltheater, Mannheim, Germany.
A Modicum of Truth, The Arches, Glasgow.

2002

Of Course It's A Journey, University of Hull @ Scarborough.
Where Have They Hidden All the Answers? National Review of Live Art/The Arches, Glasgow.
Leave No Trace, Wickham Theatre, Bristol.
A Tiny Moment of Pleasure, Tramway, Glasgow.

2001

Pills for Modern Living, InBetween Time/Arnolfini, Bristol.
Believe the Worst, Komedia, Brighton.

2000

Class of '76, Chuckery Infant School, Walsall.
The Secret Hippie Piece, TransEuropa festival, Hildesheim, Germany.
Arizona, Phoenix Arts, Leicester.
Where from Here, Roadmender, Northampton.

1999

What Happens If..., Leeds Met Studio Theatre.
Hang Up, Arnolfini, Bristol.

1998

Senseless, Arnolfini, Bristol.
Saved, BAC, London.

1997

Shallow Water, Ferens Art Gallery, Hull.
On Pleasure, ITV/The South Bank Show.
Experiment Zero (touring version), Nuffield Theatre, Lancaster.

1996

With The Light On, Showroom Cinema, Sheffield.
Candletable, Site Gallery/Quarterlight Festival, Sheffield.
Barcode, Bucknall Austin building/Quarterlight Festival, Sheffield.
The Killing Show, The Workstation/Lovebytes Festival, Sheffield.
Experiment Zero (installation), The Workstation/Quarterlight Festival, Sheffield.
Experiment Zero (performance), Site Galery, Sheffield.

1995

Testcard, The Workstation, Sheffield.

Notes

1. Third Angel, Third Angel website, available at http://www.thirdangel.co.uk/about.php (accessed 29 September 2008).
2. Third Angel, op cit.
3. Rachel Walton, interview with the author, 4 May 2007.
4. Third Angel, op cit.
5. Alex Kelly, interview with the author, 4 May 2007.
6. Walton, interview with the author, 4 May 2007.
7. Kelly, interview with the author, 4 May 2007.
8. Ibid.
9. Ibid.
10. Third Angel, notebook, 2006.
11. Walton, interview with the author, 4 May 2007.
12. Ibid.

6
Delirium
In Rehearsal with theatre O
Helen Freshwater

This chapter focuses upon the development of theatre O's *Delirium*, which takes Dostoevsky's epic novel *The Brothers Karamazov* (1880) as its starting point. The project was a considerable 'step-up' for the company's founders and co-artistic directors, Joseph Alford and Carolina Valdés, who established theatre O in 2000 after having worked together since meeting at Jacques Lecoq's school in Paris in 1996. *Delirium* represented an opportunity to build upon the success of their earlier productions – *Three Dark Tales* (2000), *The Argument* (2003) and *Astronaut* (2005) – and was an important part of their effort to realise the transition from small to mid-scale company. It gave theatre O an opportunity to deal with source material of much greater complexity and density than the devised domestic dramas generated by the company in their earlier productions. It also provided a means to capitalise upon the promising collaboration with playwright Enda Walsh, forged at the National Theatre Studio during their joint work between 2004 and 2006 on *Five Moral Agents* (2006).

The development of *Delirium* was a new departure for both Walsh and theatre O. Although both parties had found their earlier collaboration on *Five Moral Agents* exciting and productive, *Delirium* was an altogether more ambitious project. Walsh's scripts – which include *Disco Pigs* (1996), *Chatroom* (2005) and *The Walworth Farce* (2007) – had been delivered to the companies producing them before rehearsals began, and so the experience of writing during the rehearsal process was to be a new one for Walsh. Having a writer involved in a show's development, scripting their work, was also new for Alford and Valdés.

The establishment and negotiation of any new collaborative relationship necessarily involves questions of authority and ownership, and any theatre company seeking to devise a show with a writer for the first time will need to address a series of challenging questions. Whose creative vision will be the most important? Who will take the final decisions on the form and content of the production? Who is going to be named as the author of the piece on the show's publicity, or on the script if publication is planned? Who will own the copyright and the rights to future performance? The answers to these questions are obviously hugely important to all concerned and, as Deirdre Heddon and Jane Milling observe in *Devising Performance*, the commercial structures of publishing and publicity still tend to work on the assumption that a creative work will have a single, named author, which militates against recognition of performers' collective contribution to devised work. In consequence, as they demonstrate, there are many examples of fraught and sometimes difficult relationships between writers and theatre companies in the history of the development of devising (Heddon and Milling, 2006, pp. 42–4 and 109–16).

These questions of authority and ownership are thrown into particularly sharp relief when the source material is a canonical nineteenth-century novel – long celebrated as a literary masterpiece – and one of the parties involved is an established playwright, whilst the other is a company known for the accomplished physicality of their work and commitment to devising – a mode of production which has been described, amongst other things, as 'the embodiment of the death of the author' (Heddon and Milling, 2006, p. 5). Indeed, much has been made of the challenge that 'physical theatre' – such as theatre O's – purportedly presents to the traditional dominance of the scripted word in British theatre. Dymphna Callery, for example, argues that physical theatre privileges knowledge that may be primarily – or even exclusively – understood through the body, as the title of her book *Through the Body: A Practical Guide to Physical Theatre* puts it (Callery, 2001). Others have gone further. Ana Sanchez-Colberg not only links physical theatre's focus upon the corporeal to a 'devaluation of language', but also extends this point to suggest that this is generated by the wider cultural belief that language can be used to control and constrain (Sanchez-Colberg, 1996, pp. 41–2). Within this ideological framework, moving 'beyond words' often seems to imply challenging the imposition of authoritarian power, giving expression to the unsaid and the unsayable, and eliminating unconscious physical habits that deform the body's movement (see Murray, 2003, pp. 72–8 and Callery, 2001, p. 3).

Still, none of this necessarily means that work which is labelled 'physical theatre' by critics and reviewers – or indeed devised work – is necessarily 'anti-literary' or 'anti-text'. Many well-known British theatre companies whose work has been given the 'physical theatre' tag – such as Complicite and Frantic Assembly – have used existing play scripts, as well as creating adaptations of novels and short stories. Moreover, Alford made it clear to me that he certainly did not equate devising with 'the death of the author'.[1] As we shall see, theatre O's relationship to the novel, and to the text being produced by Walsh, was a complex one. But before I discuss these relationships, I need to describe the scope of my observation of this process, to assess whether *Delirium* can properly be considered to be a devised piece, and to outline some of the limitations of what I am able to say about the process of its development.

Theatre O generously gave me unlimited access to their rehearsal time, and I was able to view over 80 hours of the company's work on *Delirium* between the start of January and the end of March 2008. The development process for *Delirium* included four weeks with the performers in January 2008, followed by a three-week break from rehearsal to concentrate on writing and work on the design. The cast then came together again for a second rehearsal phase of five weeks (spending the last four of these in one of the Barbican's rehearsal rooms) and a week's technical rehearsal at the Laban Centre in Deptford before the opening at the West Yorkshire Playhouse at the start of April. The show was then booked to tour to the Lighthouse in Poole in April, the Nuffield in Southampton in May, and the Abbey, Northern Stage and the Barbican in Autumn 2008.

My observation of the company's work began on the first morning of rehearsals at the start of January 2008. On this first day, I was unsure about whether an analysis of the development process behind *Delirium* would belong in a book about devised performance. As Heddon and Milling point out in *Devising Performance*, devising is usually thought of as 'a mode of work in which *no* script – neither written play-text nor performance score – exists prior to the work's creation by the company' (2006, p. 3, italics in original) and, at this stage, I wondered whether *Delirium* would fall into this category. Walsh was already working on first drafts of some scenes, and a large part of the initial discussion with the performers that first morning was dedicated to Alford and Walsh's description and explanation of the decisions already taken about the style and structure of the piece. Though Valdés initially had the idea for an adaptation of *The Brothers Karamazov*, and was clearly heavily involved in discussions before the beginning of rehearsals (and then behind the scenes during them), she operated primarily as a performer in the rehearsal room.

A passing acquaintance with Dostoevsky's final novel will make it clear why Walsh, Valdés and Alford had taken some major decisions about the content and structure of the piece before going into rehearsal. *The Brothers Karamazov* is both stylistically diverse and notoriously convoluted, containing numerous digressions and subplots. Whilst its central focus rests on the four eponymous brothers (Dmitri, Ivan, Alyosha and the illegitimate and unacknowledged Smerdyakov), it also spends a lot of time on the stories of several minor characters, including the monk Father Zosima, the officer Captain Snegiryov, and his son Ilyusha. The novel also has ambitious intellectual and philosophical aspirations, as it examines the nature of truth, reason and free will. A profoundly spiritual work, it presents the brothers' struggles with Christian faith and doubt, as it contrasts the fervent religious belief of the youngest son Alyosha with Ivan's nihilistic atheism and Dmitri's base sensualism. Dostoevksy places his characters in situations of extreme emotional pressure. The novel explores the Karamavoz brothers' complicity in the murder of their father Fyodor, who neglected

Figure 15   Clive Mendus as Fyodor, Dominic Burdess as Ivan and Nick Lee as Dmitri in rehearsal. Photo by Helen Freshwater.

them all in childhood. Several love triangles provide romantic interest, including competition between Fyodor and Dmitri for the affections of the slippery Grushenka, and Dmitri's unhappy engagement to proud Katerina, with whom Ivan is in love.

Given the size and scope of the novel it is quite understandable that Walsh, Valdés and Alford had decided to take some decisions about the focus of the show before the start of rehearsals. But some of these decisions were substantial ones. Major elements of the book were to be completely absent, including the story of the Captain and his son. They had decided that the identity of Fyodor's murderer was never to be brought into question, thus sidestepping one of the book's main preoccupations. The performers were to be playing a single character each throughout the show, and would be on stage constantly, establishing a convention which, it was hoped, would communicate both a sense of entrapment and the characters' intense involvement with each other's lives. Walsh and Alford also indicated that they wanted the show to engage with the religious debates central to the book; and that they hoped these ideas would be expressed with an immediacy that would suggest that they had only just occurred to the characters.

Evidently, a lot of work had been done by the first day in rehearsal, and the critical issue here would seem to be when 'the work's creation by the company' – as Heddon and Milling put it – might be deemed to have begun. It is certainly possible to argue that the show's development and devising started long before I began observing the company on the first day of rehearsals at the start of January 2008. In fact, Valdés first had the idea for the show in August 2005. The project was fully cast and programmed – with the production and creative teams in place – by March 2007, but its start was delayed when the company heard that their application for Arts Council funding had been unsuccessful. After hearing that their re-application had been successful in July 2007, Alford, Valdés and Walsh met for an initial writing week together, when they discussed their approach to the book, including the themes they were interested in exploring and which characters they were likely to focus upon. Alford and Walsh met on a weekly basis to discuss their ideas for the show between July 2007 and January 2008, and also met with Rowan Williams, the Archbishop of Canterbury (who was completing his book, *Dostoevsky: Language, Faith and Fiction* (2008)) to discuss the adaptation during this period. In November 2007 they spent a week on the structure of the piece with Walsh.

Suggesting that the show's development process started in July 2007, when Alford, Valdés and Walsh began to work in earnest on the content of the piece together, would however risk underestimating the significance of the development of shared working practices which began much earlier than 2005. Many of the cast and crew, for example, had worked together before. Lucien Macdougall studied at Lecoq at the same time as Alford and Valdés, and performed with the company in *Three Dark Tales* and *Five Moral Agents*. Choreographer Eva Vilamitjana had appeared in *Astronaut* and worked on the choreography for *Three Dark Tales* and *The Argument*. Alford had directed Dominic Burdess before in *Arsenic and Old Lace* (2005), and had met the assistant director, Kate Wasserberg, whilst performing in Walsh's adaptation of Brecht's *How Much is Your Iron?* at the Young Vic in 2006. Animator and illustrator Paddy Molloy had worked with the company during a week's workshop at the Barbican in 2006, and stage manager Lucy McMahon worked with the company during the tour of *Astronaut*. The importance and impact of these earlier collaborations and contacts upon the process of devising cannot be overstated. The fact that most of the people involved had prior knowledge of each other's working methods is highly significant in terms of the speedy development of a shared language in rehearsal.

There are also definite thematic connections between this project and theatre O's earlier work. Both *The Argument* and *Astronaut* are placed in the domestic realm and explore the experience of family. They present us with childhood experiences and examine how these influence our lives as adults, showing us people battling for identity and for space, struggling with profound loneliness as they live in close proximity to others. They portray extreme emotions, produced by extraordinary circumstances. Failure in communication is central to both pieces. These themes are present in *Delirium*, which is also about a family, albeit an extremely unusual one. The brothers of Dostoevsky's title are acutely aware of their familial bonds, but they are effectively strangers: they have little or no shared history.

All of the above indicates how difficult it can be to identify the moment when a company begins work on a particular project. But it does not provide an answer to the question of whether *Delirium* can be considered a devised work. If we are happy to use Heddon and Milling's criteria for devising – 'a mode of work in which *no* script – neither written play-text nor performance score – exists prior to the work's creation by the company', then perhaps the deciding factor would be who we might consider 'the company' to be. In theatre O's case, is it just the artistic directors – the only constant since the company's establishment? Or perhaps 'the company' should include all of the cast and crew who came together to work on *Delirium* in January 2008? If we define 'the company' as the former, then *Delirium* is certainly a devised piece; if the latter, perhaps it is not.

Still, I put these questions of definition aside as I became immersed in the show's development and it rapidly became plain that the performers would have a central creative role. During discussion on the first day of rehearsals, Alford insisted several times that the style for the show was not yet fixed, that the performers would have a great deal of free rein, and that Walsh would be watching their improvisations and responding to the way that they developed their characters.[2] The importance of the performers' contributions became evident during the first two weeks of rehearsal, as they explored and established their characters first in improvisations around *commedia dell'arte* stock characters and scenarios, and then through improvisations which placed the characters in a series of situations – suggested by the performers – which would not appear in the final piece. This is a strategy that the company have pursued in the development of earlier productions – Valdés explained that they expect to return to these improvisations during the tour to keep the show fresh.

Having reassured myself that this was devised work, I now found myself concerned with the difficulties and limitations inherent in any attempt to assess and survey the process of devising. Although I was fortunate enough to be able to view many hours of the company's work in rehearsal, it quickly became clear that I could not avoid missing large tranches of the show's development. Even if I had been at every rehearsal, I could not have seen every moment of the development of *Delirium*. I often had to make choices about what to watch, as the group regularly divided to focus upon different scenes and aspects of the production. For example, one afternoon Paddy Molloy, the animator, was recording Clive Mendus's movement as he performed as Fyodor; Lucien Macdougall was working with Gus Macmillan on the sound for a series of puppetry interludes for his character Smerdyakov; assistant director Kate Wasserberg explored a scene between Katerina and Ivan with Valdés and Dominic Burdess (with Aideen Malone looking on, taking notes on lighting); and Alford worked with Nick Lee and Julie Bower on one of their scenes as Dmitri and Grushenka. Later in the process the company was also joined by the choreographer, Vilamitjana, who often worked separately on movement and dance with members of the cast.

A huge amount of work was also being done outside of the rehearsal room. As well as the design of lighting and set, realisation of the animation and sourcing of costumes, it became apparent that Alford and

Walsh regularly phoned each other to discuss the show in the evenings. Moreover, as the development period progressed, there were often times when following the performers' discussion of the show could be difficult. The adoption of allusive titles for the individual scenes was sometimes confusing and the performers' use of nicknames for movement sequences could be all but impossible to decipher. These problems are nothing, however, to the difficulties inherent in describing the humour which permeated the development process during the first phase of rehearsals, which had a significant role to play in the development of *Delirium*. The ironic and light-hearted tone of some of the comments made in the rehearsal room is not necessarily perceptible once they are transcribed. Here it seems important to note that though all descriptions of performance have to negotiate its ephemerality, the fragments of performance which circulate during the devising process seem, if anything, to have an even greater fragility and transience. Many will be discarded, and never find form or a place in memory through repetition. And, without ever having had public exposure, they can seem curiously insubstantial.

One final caveat about the following comments on the development of *Delirium*. The process that I describe below was certainly not an ideal one for theatre O, as the project was realised on a very tight budget. The company secured 30 per cent of the money they needed from the project's co-commissioners, the Barbican and the Abbey Theatre, and 50 per cent from the Arts Council, as well as grants from the Alan Cadbury Charitable Trust and support from the Laban Centre and the Pushkin House Trust. These, however, did not cover the original budget, and the company took a difficult decision to cut costs. The primary result of this decision was Alford's inclusion in the show as a performer: something that he and Valdés had originally wanted to avoid. These financial constraints also had an impact upon the development process's timetable. Alford explained that they would, ideally, have chosen to leave a number of months between the first and second blocks of rehearsal, but that this had not been possible. These pragmatic considerations certainly had a huge impact upon the process, and will, no doubt, have shaped the piece's final form. In consequence I am very aware that I am not describing a process which the company would consider to be ideal; and the comments which follow must be taken as speculative, rather than authoritative, given my inevitably limited view of the show's development.

These qualifications notwithstanding, some aspects of the production's development were striking. The company's stated attitude towards the process of adaptation and their approach to the novel could even be seen as being provocative. Alford and Valdés described the piece on the company's website as 'theatre O and Enda Walsh's free and outrageous adaptation of Fyodor Dostoevsky's *The Brothers Karamazov*'.[3] Alford reflects on this approach in the company's blog as he describes meetings with Walsh in October 2007:

> We're aiming to really capture the spirit and energy of the novel without feeling constrained or held back by 'doing the book' on stage. We feel that would be both impossible and foolish. The stage (obviously) is a different form and therefore demands a different way of looking at things, a different way of telling a story. We don't want to be forcing stuff in 'because it's in the book'. We need to make something that stands up on its own.[4]

This approach is signalled by their choice to name the production *Delirium*, rather than making an explicit reference in its title to *The Brothers Karamazov*. Instead, the title signals the company's interest in responding to the disorientating and feverish qualities of the book.

In fact, during discussion of the novel on the first day of rehearsals, it became evident that the performers shared an ambivalent attitude towards the novel. Most of the cast admitted that although they had been excited by the extraordinary range of characters that it contains, and the extremity and intensity of these characters' behaviours and experiences, they had found reading it a challenge, having struggled with its length and the difficulty of following the narrative. Walsh supported this critical perspective, stating that he had also found the novel frustrating to read. Citing its 'terrible plotting', he observed that he would not be treating the novel with particular respect or reverence, as he noted that when he first read it he thought: 'we can do something better than this!'[5]

This ambivalent relationship was highlighted on the one occasion when I saw the company gathered together to read a scene from the novel. This scene, in which Grushenka and Katerina first meet, generated considerable hilarity. Dostoevsky's description of Grushenka – the novel's alluring femme fatale – certainly is bizarre:

> Softly she lowered herself into an armchair, softly rustling her ample black silk dress, and delicately wrapping her plump neck, white as foam, and her wide shoulders in an expensive black woollen shawl. ... Her complexion was very white, with a pale rosy tint

high on her cheeks. The shape of her face was too broad, perhaps, and her lower jaw even protruded a bit. Her upper lip was thin, and her more prominent lower lip was twice as full and seemed a little swollen.

(Dostoevsky, 2004, p. 148)

The uncontrollable laughter which greeted this description could hardly be interpreted as a sign that the company were in awe of Dostoevsky's work. Having been asked to comment on this hilarity, however, Alford noted that the respect he had for the novel should not be underestimated. He argued that he *was* in awe of it as a piece of work, and that the subversive approach that the company were adopting towards it was 'an essential part of making something that is ours and not a version of his'.[6]

As rehearsals continued, the delicate balance between subversion and respect often seemed to tip towards the latter. The novel went on to function as a source of authority in the rehearsal room, despite occasional acknowledgement that it should not govern the choices being taken. At different moments in the development process almost all of the performers, as well as Alford, Valdés and Wasserberg, made reference to the book to support or justify decisions taken about the show's content, structure and style. Performers frequently proposed changes to lines and action on the basis that they more effectively 'reflected' the novel. Mendus, for example, changed the script in the scene where Fyodor describes abusing his first wife in order to make it obvious that he is disappointed that nothing happens when he spits on a crucifix, explaining that he felt that it better reflected Fyodor's behaviour in the novel, whilst Alford decided that Alyosha should faint in response to Fyodor's speech: 'as it's in the book'.[7]

Yet returning to the novel as a source of inspiration and information was not an easy choice. As already noted, *The Brothers Karamazov* is a famously convoluted novel and includes some tortuously complex plotting. During the second week of rehearsal the company was preoccupied with the question of how much information the audience needed about the characters' histories, and how best to represent the complex set of financial transactions that Dostoevsky uses to tie Dmitri to his now-unwanted fiancée, Katerina. Walsh expressed concern about overloading audiences with complex information in the first few scenes, whilst some of the performers experimented with forms of exposition that made the labyrinthine twists in the novel's sequence of transactions explicit. Lee, for example, presented an improvisation to the company in which Dmitri struggled to explain the situation with Katerina to Alyosha. Moving in close, he addressed the company directly. Beginning his description in the third person, he pulled crumpled notes and receipts from his pockets and gave each of the company a piece to scrutinise. He repeated the gesture of pushing hair out of his eyes, as though he was trying to see more clearly. Then, setting these scraps of paper out on the floor, he began to shift them around to illustrate the movement of money, effectively communicating Dmitri's increasing confusion and frustration with the difficulty of providing a straightforward explanation. This improvisation's use of a paper trail did not find a place in the show, but the anxiety it expressed remained present throughout the process. Members of the company were still debating whether or not the audience would understand the basis of Dmitri's debt to Katerina well into the final weeks of rehearsal at the Barbican.

These concerns were exacerbated by the fact that the company were very aware of one of the main problems that all adaptations have to anticipate. Their audiences might include people who had never read the novel – who might 'glaze over' when confronted with all this information – as well as those who might be attracted to the show because they have a special – and potentially proprietorial – interest in Dostoevsky. For example, the decision to bring Ivan and Katerina together in a romantic clinch towards the end of the show was taken in the knowledge that, as Alford put it: 'this is where all the Dostoevsky buffs say "isn't Ivan meant to be with the devil?"'.[8] Inevitably, the cast and crew fell into the latter category. I was the only person in the rehearsal room not to have read the novel. This was partly because I did not have the time to do so before the rehearsals began, but it was also a conscious decision: it allowed me to consider whether the developing performance seemed to be coherent on its own terms.

Intriguingly, there was a division amongst some members of the cast, Walsh and Alford about the importance of some of the traditional signals of this coherence. During discussion in the first day of rehearsals, some of the performers were keen to establish where and when the action would be taking place. Walsh and Alford agreed that the setting was roughly present day, in a suburban hinterland or a kind of purgatory, but avoided making reference to a specific location or cultural milieu. This indeterminacy continued throughout the process. Sometimes this appeared to be a definite principle, at others it seemed that the company simply did not have time to address the issues raised by the transposition of the novel's action from nineteenth-century

Russia. A brief early discussion about the wisdom of keeping Russian names was quickly displaced by the company's increasing familiarity with them; whilst the decision was actively taken to replace obviously Russian place names with European locations with less cultural baggage. This compromise seemed to me to be indicative of the company's broader relationship with the novel. On the one hand, Alford and Valdés insisted on the 'free and outrageous' nature of the adaptation, asserting that they had no intention of 'doing the book' on stage. Yet this approach was adopted in the interests of better serving the novel's 'spirit and energy': a form of faithfulness realised through betrayal. In rehearsal, the novel was treated with both subversive humour and respectful deference.

The company's relationship to the text being provided by Walsh was also complex. Walsh delivered the first section of the script at the end of the second week of rehearsals, and a revealing discussion about the status and function of this text followed the initial read through. At first, Walsh encouraged the performers to grasp the lines of information about relationships and money, but to keep everything 'open ... messy ... not too authored'. Burdess responded by noting that performers often have a tendency to deliver a script word-for-word once it has been provided, and asked whether Walsh wanted the performers to play with the words. Walsh responded by encouraging the performers to first read the scene as written, and then to 'loosen it up, fuck it up, find other words for it'. Alford seconded this, urging them to learn the lines and then to play with them. Walsh then concluded the discussion – with immaculate comic timing that I cannot do justice to here – with an observation that the performers should approach his agent if they wanted to make any changes to the script.

At first, the emphasis upon reproducing the script word-for-word seemed to dominate. During the first run-through of Act I in the third week of rehearsals, stage manager McMahon acted as prompt; and in week four, whilst watching Wasserberg working with Burdess and Valdés on a scene between Ivan and Katerina, I witnessed sustained attention being given to the detail of the text, as Wasserberg proposed that the performers' interpretations respond to the order of the words. When asked whether these approaches might be interpreted as deference to the script, Alford observed that having a prompt during a run-through should not be seen as indicative of a reverent attitude towards the text, but that it was simply a pragmatic method of keeping the company together as they worked through scenes that they were still unfamiliar with. Commenting on Wasserberg's approach, he argued that he felt that it was important to first understand the potential and possibilities of the script, and that it functioned as a structure enabling experimentation, in much the same way as rules and constraints can be used to generate useful material in improvisations. Alford also paid tribute to Walsh at this point, arguing that he knew few writers who could manage to be responsive to improvisations whilst maintaining the distinctiveness of their own voice, and who would be prepared to relinquish the traditional authority associated with the writer's role.

Certainly, as the process developed, it became clear that the company was playing with the script as Walsh had suggested after the first read through in the second week. Perhaps the most significant change occurred at the end of the company's first week back together after the three-week writing break. Having watched a video of an earlier run-through of the first act the night before, Alford and Valdés arrived in rehearsal planning to cut all of Alford's lines as Alyosha until the final scene of Act I – without first discussing this with Walsh. The company spent the day exploring the consequences of this tactic and decided that it produced a useful emphasis upon Alyosha's confusion, and the way in which other characters used his silence as a vessel for their confessions. This radical cut was representative of the company's willingness to cut lines, physical sequences, and even whole scenes, right up until the final week before the technical rehearsal.

Maintaining a productive balance between this responsive flexibility and the production of a coherent piece for public consumption was central to the process. In the second week of rehearsal, Alford remarked to me that the challenge of exploring the style and the world of the piece without making the show – of finding an appropriate theatrical language without fixing the material they were working on – was the biggest the company had yet faced. His willingness to make drastic changes, and to leave aspects of the production open until late in the process, was perceived in different ways by the performers. Bower, for example, noted in the first week of the second phase of rehearsals that she found it amazing how much of the production was still in flux. I found myself feeling similar surprise two weeks later, watching Alford moving numerous pieces of paper around on the floor as the company discussed the possible sequence of scenes, and again as I realised that the company was still without a script for the final scene as they began the final week of rehearsal prior to the move to the technical rehearsals at the Laban Centre. By contrast, at the end of this week, Mendus commented that he considered the show to be relatively far on in its development, and that

Figure 16 Joseph Alford as Alyosha in rehearsal, March 2008. Photo by Helen Freshwater.

it was certainly more fixed than he would expect a Complicite show to be at this stage (Mendus shared classes with Simon McBurney, Complicite's artistic director, during training at the Lecoq School in Paris, and performed in several of their shows, including *The Visit* (1989), *The Street of Crocodiles* (1992) and *Measure for Measure* (2003)). But the fact that the script for the final scene did not arrive until a couple of days before the company moved to technical rehearsals does, I think, indicate that the company were working with an unusually high level of flexibility.

Figure 17   Julie Bower as Grushenka in rehearsal, March 2008. Photo by Helen Freshwater. The detail of this scene, in which Grushenka packs to leave, did not make it into the show.

The inclusivity of the space being provided for discussion and analysis during the early phase of rehearsals also struck me as exceptional. Alford welcomed contributions, and on occasion actively sought comments on run-throughs and improvisations from everyone in the rehearsal room, including not only animator Molloy and composer Macmillan, but others who might, in other circumstances, be considered to be outside the creative process: namely the stage manager McMahon, and myself. This approach is evidence of the company's commitment to the notion of the ensemble, and accords with the following statement, which appears on their website:

> The one constant, however, is the idea of the 'company', the ensemble, the collaboration. The successful makeup of the group is often the hardest and most painful thing to achieve. If done well, however, then half the battle is already won. The absolute commitment of everyone involved is essential. That commitment brings an ownership of the work that will bring unparalleled results. We are interested in the actor as creator, not as puppet. Quite simply, theatre O is only as good and as exciting as the sum of the people who are involved in the creation of the company's work.[9]

Nonetheless, theatre O is not claiming to work with the kind of non-hierarchical model of collective authority explored by theatre companies such as Red Ladder and Monstrous Regiment during the 1960s and 1970s, and Alford's authority as artistic director of the project was clear throughout the process. Indeed, the beginning of the second phase of rehearsals saw a distinct shift in tone. Instead of following improvisations with discussion and feedback, Alford took a much more traditional directorial approach, following the presentation of scenes with notes to individual performers, and at times selecting music designed to indicate the rhythm he was hoping to achieve.

The centrality of Alford's creative vision became striking when he began to illustrate the sound effects which would occur in particular scenes. In the first week of the second phase of rehearsal, for example, Alford concluded a run-through of a scene in which Smerdyakov records Ivan's pronouncements on religion by vocalising noises that suggested that the sound effects at this moment would evoke the voices distorted by rewinding of the tape, morphing into a drunken cry of 'Grushenka!' from Fyodor. So, although several of the performers contributed to the form and content of the sound effects, and the concluding animation sequence, there was a strong sense that only Alford knew how all of these separate layers of signification would fit together in the staged production.

For those involved, the risk involved in keeping so much open until the last minute was noticeably challenging. During the company's last day at the Barbican before the start of the technical rehearsals, Walsh commented that he had found the process nerve-racking at times, observing that although he felt confident that the company had 'done justice' to the characters and the novel's engagement with religious debate, he was feeling an unusually high level of anxiety about the opening at the West Yorkshire Playhouse. For Walsh, this anxiety focused upon a sense that he still didn't know 'what it [the play] is', a situation which he compared with the more conventional – and reassuring – process of producing a script, delivering it to a company, having a close relationship with the director and then 'recognising the final thing'.[10] Certainly, as I left the company as they moved into the week of technical rehearsals at the Laban Centre, I had a strong sense that the production due to be staged for the first time just over a week later – complete with animation, lighting, costumes and sound – might be all but unrecognisable to me. Moreover, from Alford's perspective, the moment when the production goes in front of an audience is far from being 'the final thing'. It is just the beginning of the process.

Watching theatre O at work, it became apparent that, although the answers to the questions about authority and ownership I listed at the start of this chapter may be of vital importance to those involved in a production, they often only provide us with very partial information about the way in which these issues have been negotiated during a show's development. Alford was undoubtedly 'in charge' in the rehearsal room, but the success of the show was ultimately dependent upon the creative contribution being made by the ensemble, and the publicity for the show – which described it as being 'created by theatre O, written by Enda Walsh' – highlighted the input of both company and playwright.[11] Nevertheless, the title of the script for the production, *Delirium: After The Brothers Karamazov* (published in 2008) signals the work's debt to Dostoevsky's novel rather than to the performers. Still, these are only the outward signs of a set of collaborative relationships which were inevitably much more subtle than these labels and phrases imply. In fact, the material which made it into the show itself – as I saw it performed at the Barbican – provided more useful opportunities for reflection upon the complexities and compromises involved in processes of collaborative adaptation and storytelling.

The production presented a whirling storm of movement, sound and argument, fully realising the delirium of the title. But in the middle of this mix of exaggerated gesture, Punch and Judy style puppetry, and aggressive use of sound, audiences are presented with two characters – Alyosha and Smerdyakov – who are busy trying to preserve the words of a respected teacher. Alyosha resorts to using a sock puppet to ventriloquise Father Zosima's homilies, and Smerdyakov avidly tapes Ivan's eloquent attacks upon religious belief. But during the production these characters move beyond obsession with the faithful recall and accurate reconstruction of the sacred or authoritative word. In the final scenes, both Smerdyakov and Alyosha find their own voices in two long monologues, whose static, still delivery was in stark contrast to the assertive physicality and violent verbal exchanges that characterised the rest of the show. The delirium halts as the audience are confronted first by Smerdyakov, who presents his own terrible history, backed by an allusive arrangement of animated images. The catalogue of abuse he describes builds from the particular to the general, from his own story to a description of a world of full of pain and injustice, as finally he conflates the religious and the personal: 'God has left this house but it is always someone's face! It is His face! His words! His needs! His abuse! Father's sin!' (Walsh/theatre O, 2008, p. 66). Here the words of the father are associated with oppression and abuse of power, but the following final scene presents us with an alternative reading of the power of the word. In a quiet, reflective scene of simple, direct address, Alyosha imagines a future beyond the apocalypse, in which we can find hope and begin again. After his description of the world's destruction he pauses, and then continues: 'But still, there's a word inside all of this heartache. And it seems it should be lost for ever, that it could never be mined from a world wanting to end ... but the word is there. ... It's a tiny faith ... an unbreakable goodness ... a "hope"' (p. 67). So, the production does not leave us with Smerdyakov's angry rejection of the authority of the father and the word, but with the word 'hope', an affecting image of a happy childhood, and an impossible future history for the Karamazovs. The tension between the two monologues provides a useful starting point for thinking through the promise and challenges inherent in experiments in devising which bring together theatre artists who work primarily with the word and with the body. It seems that the authority of the word will always need to be negotiated but there is hope that such collaborations can make it live anew.

Chronology of productions

Three Dark Tales (2000) Windsor Arts Centre, then national and international tours.
The Argument (2003) Theatre Royal, Plymouth, then national and international tours.
Astronaut (2005) Trinity Arts Centre, Tunbridge, then national and international tours.
Five Moral Agents (2006) National Theatre Studio. London.
Delirium (2008) West Yorkshire Playhouse, then national and international tours.
For more on the company's work, see www.theatreo.co.uk.

Notes

1. Joseph Alford, personal communication, 16 May 2008.
2. Alford, comments in rehearsals, 7 January 2008.
3. theatre O, www.everythingispermitted.co.uk/home.html (accessed 8 May 2008).
4. Alford, www.theatreo.co.uk/bl_O_g/, 21 October 2007 (accessed 12 May 2008).
5. Enda Walsh, in conversation in rehearsals, 7 January 2008.
6. Alford, communication with the author, 16 May 2008.
7. Alford, comments in rehearsals, 17 March 2008.
8. Alford, comments in rehearsals, 19 March 2008.
9. www.theatreo.co.uk/main.html (accessed 8 May 2008).
10. Walsh, in conversation in rehearsals, 31 March 2008.
11. See www.barbican.org.uk/theatre/event-detail.asp?ID=7615; www.abbeytheatre.ie/2008season/delerium.html (accessed 9 August 2008).

7
Clash and Consensus in Shunt's 'Big Shows' and the *Lounge*

Alex Mermikides

Shunt is unusual in both its organisational and creative activities. At a time when most new companies form economical 'core and pool' company structures Shunt operates as a collective of ten artists. Most of the artists met as students on the Central School of Speech and Drama's Master's course in Advanced Theatre Practice (Serena Bobowski, Gemma Brockis, Lizzie Clachan, Louise Mari, Hannah Ringham, David Rosenberg, Andrew Rutland, Mischa Twitchin and Heather Uprichard, with Layla Rosa joining them later). While most new companies find rehearsal space where they can and tour to existing venues, Shunt set up a permanent base in which to create and perform its work. Arch 12a, Gales Gardens, Bethnal Green (known to the company as 'the Arch'), was a disused railway arch which the company renovated as a rehearsal and performance space. Here they produced *The Ballad of Bobby Francois* (1999–2001) and *Dance Bear Dance* (2002–3), as well as the bi-monthly Shunt *Cabaret*. Once the possibilities of working in this space had been exhausted, the company moved to a massive disused wine warehouse underneath London Bridge Station. The Shunt Vaults have been home to another two shows, *Tropicana* (2004–5) and *Amato Saltone Starring Kittens and Wade* (2005–6) and their most recent project, the *Shunt Lounge*. Shunt's refusal to blindly adopt established practices or to compromise its ambition in the face of economic restraints testifies to its independence of vision.

This originality is also evident in its large-scale shows, which for now I will describe as site-specific promenade performances, though these terms do not do justice to their inspired use of non-theatre space or to the atmospheric and immersive experience they create for their audiences. Although these are usually based on known stories or events – the plane crash in the Andes for *Bobby Francois*, the Gunpower Plot for *Dance Bear Dance*, the fiction of Cornell Woolrich (author of *Rear Window*) for *Amato Saltone* – any relation in the big shows to the source text is oblique. The original text provides thematic, atmospheric and imagistic inspiration rather than a clear story line. The 'scenes' (a term I use loosely) follow each other without obvious chronological or causal sequence. This is not to say that there are not moments when a strand of events suggest that there is a deep, if hidden, structure: in *Tropicana*, for example, we meet a lift operator who appears again in a lift cage that hurtles (horizontally) through the long corridors as we sit in the almost pitch-black side rooms; we follow his funeral procession and are fed sandwiches at the wake. How this character relates to the distressed scientists and the showgirls that stalk the space is not immediately clear. Yet this does not seem to concern the audiences, for whom this is an experience in which structure and coherence is determined not by narrative events but by a physical and emotional journey.

For those familiar with such shows, the *Shunt Lounge* – which looks, at first glance, like club night in a bar with the added novelty of experimental performances – might seem an illogical, even unwise, new direction: a wasted opportunity to capitalise on the new audience attracted by the accolades that greeted the early shows – *The Ballad of Bobby Francois* won a Herald Angel and a Total Theatre Award; *Dance Bear Dance* received *Time Out*'s 'Live' Award and an 'Empty Space' Award. However, the *Shunt Lounge* is an innovative but ultimately logical response by this particular company to artistic and economic imperatives. Moreover, in comparing the structure and principles of the *Lounge* with those of the 'big shows', this chapter will raise issues that are pertinent to all devising companies – even though the distinctive nature of these projects presented significant challenges in terms of the research and the inclusion of this work in a book about devising.

What this chapter cannot offer, for example, is a neat narrative of how a show was made. This is not only because the nebulous nature of the *Lounge* (the only project coinciding with the research for this book), together with restrictions on access to rehearsals, ruled out rehearsal observation. It is also because the *Shunt Lounge* can be seen as *both* a collection of performances *and* an extended creative process – though it stretches conventional definitions of both. At the same time, it could be argued that it is neither: as suggested above, the *Shunt Lounge* looks more like an unusual club night than a theatre performance. This is something that, at first, made me question whether it could right-fully be included in this book about devising. I was partly persuaded by company member Mischa Twitchin's insistence that 'the *Lounge is* the show'[1] (Twitchin, who took the Dramaturgy strand at Central, is mainly responsible for the lighting in the Shunt shows). And indeed, there are performances, by individual or sub-groups of Shunt artists as well as by guest practitioners, at almost every *Lounge* night. I was also aware that, like the Shunt Cabaret before it (which will be described more fully later), the *Lounge* can be seen as a forum for generating and developing material that may eventually inform the next group-created 'big show' and, as such, can be seen as a devising process, albeit a rather meandering one. The decisive factor, however, was the realisation that a comparison between the collective devising of the company's 'big shows' and the pattern of work they have adopted for the *Lounge* raises issues that go to the very core of what devising is about.

The *Lounge* opened on 15 September 2006 and continues to draw a crowd every Wednesday, Thursday, Friday and, since June 2007, Saturday evening. Attending the *Lounge* is an experience, as is clear from its promotional film.[2] Entering through an inconspicuous service door just outside London Bridge underground station, you negotiate a series of surprising spaces: the ticketing room with its once-elegant desks, a wood-panelled hall with mysterious numbered doors, the remains of the opening set from *Tropicana*, including a convincing replica of a lift cubicle (this has now been removed). You walk down the dramatically lit 'long corridor' with its open side rooms where installations and films are often shown. Eventually you come to the bar area with its DJ booth, mis-matched furniture, pool tables, a milk float and more pieces of past sets, all dwarfed by the sweeping brick walls and arched ceiling. The crowd socialises, explores and, particularly later in the evening, dances. From time to time there is an announcement that there will be a performance in the Arena space, or the Wake space, or in one of the studios, and a small crowd congregates to see it.

The choice of 'entertainment' is decided by individual Shunt artists who take turns to 'curate' a week or two-week period of *Lounge* evenings, selecting the performances, installations, live music, DJs and films on offer, sometimes around themes or in relation to larger festivals. The offerings often include shows created by individual Shunt artists: for example performer Hannah Ringham's *The Pigeon,* a solo performance as an anthropomorphic pigeon-woman in a grey tracksuit and crippling pink stilettos, or a series of meticulous pieces using extracts of texts from writers such as Adorno, Deleuze and Wittgenstein created by Twitchin for the Vault's smallest spaces. There are also performances by other groups: Frank Chickens, Rotozazza, Station House Opera and Motiroti are some of the more established names, but Shunt

Figure 18   The Shunt Vaults. View from the Wake Space down the Long Corridor.
Photo by Bazzachan.

welcome proposals from *Lounge* members, students and 'mavericks'.[3]
Occasionally, there are interventions in the main bar space: the *Mud
Man* series created by Shunt artist Louise Mari (who usually operates
as the writer or dramaturg in the big shows) and Shunt associate artist,
performer Nigel Barrett, in which a naked mud-caked Barrett interacted
with the visitors;[4] or a model of a Sputnik moving slowly through the
drinking area (*Laika in the Rust of Utopia*), which inspired a spontaneous
procession of *Lounge* visitors following its course through the space. It
is an exciting and unpredictable evening for those attending. What is
in it, though, for the Shunt artists?

Initially the *Lounge* was conceived as a 'bit of a holiday'.[5] The first two
years in the Vaults were an exhausting cycle of building work, rehearsals
and performances. The Shunt artists themselves undertook most of the
work required to render to the disused space habitable (which included
fitting plumbing and electricity – no mean feat given the size of the
space). This work continued as rehearsals for *Tropicana* began and the
show ran, with two shows an evening, for nine months. Rehearsals for

Amato Saltone, which opened only four months after *Tropicana* closed, took place during the run. Once *Amato Saltone* closed five months later, in March 2006, the Shunt artists were creatively and physically exhausted; it was inconceivable to go into yet another big show. However the imperative to keep the space functioning and to sustain the audience remained. Opening the bar and the venue to the public offered a solution and was, I would argue, a continuation of the company's practice. Almost every Shunt event (at both venues) has featured a bar which acts as a point of congregation and celebration, usually at the end of the performance (in *Tropicana* drinks were offered at the beginning of the show, served by disembodied arms through the panelled walls as the audience waited for the next lift and also out of the back of a hearse half-way through the show). This merging of performance and bar space is one mark of the company's distinction from established practices: Twitchin described how audience members spontaneously danced in the bar after *Dance Bear Dance*, freed to do so because 'it's not in a theatre so people's expectations were being played with.'[6]

In the same way, programming the 'entertainment' is a logical development from creating the Shunt shows. As will be described later in more detail later, these shows are immersive and mood-enhancing experiences rather than what might be described as the moving pictures of more conventional theatre. Light, sound and, above all, the geography of non-theatre spaces (the dimensions of the rooms, the existence of secret doors, the length of the corridors) are employed 'to create an audience experience that isn't passive, where you can't just sit and dissociate yourself from it'.[7] The company's long experience of creating such events, and of attracting a young, 'trendy' audience that theatre rarely reaches, has stood the company in good stead:

> Making performances that were always focussed on the audience experience has given us a very useful experience that is transferable from performances to a bar, to how to make the experience of sitting at a bar more experiential, more of an event and that's one of the key things of why this project works.[8]

Although the Shunt artists have mixed feelings about their new identity as bar managers, the *Lounge* is very successful as a bar: for example it was listed as number 25 of the 191 'star bars' in the *Independent*.[9] And it is interesting to note that the defining characteristic of Shunt's events, their experiential nature, was picked up by a bar-guide reviewer's comment that 'the *Shunt Lounge* is not about what you can buy, it's about what you can experience.'[10] The *Lounge* also offers an exciting model of how a theatre company might function economically. But in what way is it either a performance or a devising process?

To answer this we must first consider the fact that the *Lounge* provides a space (resourced and supported by Building Manager, Andrea Salazar) and an audience of up to 2000 visitors a week for Shunt artists and guests to show their own work. It is, as Twitchin suggested, a 'show', that is, a performance. Nevertheless, the *Lounge* is simultaneously a forum for *developing* as well as simply showing work, as is evidenced by the fact that some of the Shunt artists' projects find their finished form outside the venue: Gemma Brockis (usually a performer) and long-term Shunt collaborator Silvia Mercuriali created a highly original version of *Pinocchio*, which is played to audiences of up to three at a time in the back of a car careening through the streets of various cities across the world. David Rosenberg's *Contains Violence* had a full run at the Lyric Hammersmith after a series of work-in-progress showings at the *Lounge*. The fact that the *Lounge* is an ongoing project, and that the artists can (and often do) show their work more than once, gives them the opportunity to go through a process of reflection, revision and re-showing: the cyclical pattern that is at the heart of all theatre-making processes. Moreover, the *Lounge* creates what Luke Cooper (the General Manager) calls a 'sympathetic' audience, earning the very necessary right to fail that is so vital to creative processes. It does this by cleverly shifting the emphasis away from the performances and presentations – as is shown in the company's own description of the *Lounge*:

> A members' bar deep in the tunnels under London Bridge Station. ... Each week will be curated by a different Shunt artist. Some will fill the space with non-stop entertainment, some will do next to nothing. Fortunately the bar staff are more reliable.[11]

The artists are thereby let off the hook when it comes to providing 'entertainment', both in terms of presenting their own work and curating the *Lounge* (that is, selecting and supporting work by guest artists, who are likewise granted a right to fail). The membership scheme (granted on a periodic or nightly basis) also reflects this, as the audience pays for the night rather than any particular show. In fact, except for the rare interventions in the bar, the performance events are generally optional. The audience that do see the performances thus have very different expectations than they would if going to see a conventional theatre production; as Rosenberg says, 'the audience are taking much less of a risk and consequently the performance can take more of a risk.'[12]

We see, then, that the *Lounge* can be defined as a collection of processes happening in parallel. However, unless there is a degree of creative exchange between the Shunt artists and, more importantly, unless we assume that they will eventually come together to create a company show from these proto-performances, then it would be difficult to define the *Lounge* as a single devising process. This, of course, is the point for a company whose collaborative approach to process has always sought to challenge the model of the single author (though, as I will suggest shortly, the role that Rosenberg plays as director of the big shows might suggest that the company's practice is not as radical in this respect as they might claim). Some creative exchange between artists does exist: the artists see each other's work and there is a *Lounge* blog, a private online discussion group for what Cooper describes as the 'constant discourse' that Shunt requires: 'because they have this collective way of making decisions, things have to be talked about.'[13] However, with the next group project only just being announced as this chapter was being written, how the individual projects and experiences of the *Lounge* might come together is yet to be investigated (though the title of the new show, *Money*, is significant, given the economic motivation of the *Lounge* project). In the meanwhile, however, the company's decision to work as individuals creating work in parallel rather than in collaboration allows us to examine two key creative principles of devising. I will call these the clash principle, which I will illustrate through the example of the happening form, and the consensus principle as demonstrated by the notion of the ensemble.

The happening, an avant-garde form which emerged in the United States in the 1950s, provides an important precedent for the structure of the *Lounge*. In its purest form, the happening brought different artists together in what Michael Kirby calls a 'compartmented' structure, based on: 'the arrangement and contiguity of theatrical units that are completely self-contained and hermetic. No information is passed from one discrete theatrical unit – or 'compartment' to another' (Kirby, 1995, p. 5). For example, in John Cage's seminal 1952 work at the Black Mountain College:

> Cage, dressed in a black suit and tie, read a lecture on Meister Eckhart from a raised lectern at one side. ... M.C. Richards recited from a ladder. Charles Olsen and other performers 'planted' in the audience each stood up when their time came and said a line or two.

> David Tudor played the piano. Movies were projected on the
> ceiling. ... Robert Rauschenberg operated old records on a hand-
> wound phonograph, and Merce Cunningham improvised a dance
> around the audience. A dog began to follow Cunningham and was
> accepted into the presentation
>
> (Kirby, 1995, p. 19)

There is a similarity here to the structure of the *Lounge*, where the Shunt
artists work in parallel rather than in collaboration, with no particular
intention to create a sense of overall coherence. In the happening,
the resulting discordance was intentional because it subverted authorial intention, and with this, traditional notions of art as a display of
virtuosity, meaning and coherence. This is not to say that interesting
connections were not made between the separate elements: chance
and randomness open the possibility of serendipitous and surprising
conjunctions.

This compartmenting of artists and their creative contributions might
seem at odds with the characterisation of devising as a collaborative
and interrelationship practice. However, the concept of creativity that
underlies the happening structure – which I will shorthand as the 'clash'
principle – pervades much devising practice, albeit in a less radical form.
It is most obvious in the postmodern aesthetic of live art, particularly in
its favouring of fragmentary, deliberately incoherent forms. The creative
processes of such performances often foster what Tim Etchells of Forced
Entertainment calls 'a mis-seeing, a mis-hearing, a deliberate lack of
unity' (Etchells, 1999, p. 56). More broadly accepted still is the belief
that by minimising preconception or authorial intention, the devising
group allows creative friction between disparate elements and views to
spark innovation and novelty.

Shunt's employment of this principle is most obvious in the *Cabaret*,
which David Bere (2001/2) describes as '[hanging] together through the
sheer will power of its originators and the enthusiastic response of the
filled to capacity audience'. Like a traditional cabaret, it constituted a
series of disjointed acts (by Shunt artists and guests) compered by one
or more of the Shunt artists, often in bizarre guises: a compartmented
structure. This, together with the audience's goodwill (created in part
by free entry), allowed the artists to experiment with what Brockis
calls 'unfeasible' work.[14] Such material is 'unfeasible' not only because
it is experimental and often bizarre, but because it is not immediately
obvious how it might develop. Nevertheless, 'a lot of stuff from the
Cabaret ended up in the shows in a very, sometimes in a really 'whole'

[unchanged] way. Like, some people's whole acts were just lifted and ended in the show a few years later or whatever.'[15]

The principle is also evident in the creative process of the big shows, in particular the early phases when the artists 'start off putting individual ideas on the table and [say] who they want to work with and what they want the show to be about'.[16] These proposals may be verbal (the phase does include sit-down discussions), but more important are the practical presentations: sketches and demonstrations, performed either within the context of the *Cabaret* (until 2003) or as part of the rehearsal proper. Shunt member Layla Rosa (the company's aerialist) describes this activity of presenting as 'our chance to say "if I was making the show and it was an aerial show for example this is what I'd do".[17] The more unlikely and 'unfeasible' the proposals, the more useful they might be.

There comes a point in Shunt's process, as in most devising processes, when this 'free-for-all' experimental phase must be tempered with practical concerns and decision making. This is something that scholars and practitioners of devising seem to forget: the rhetoric about devising tends to emphasise what Oddey called its 'freedom of possibilities' (Oddey, 1996, p. 2) – a suspension of judgement, a softening of hierarchy and a policy of 'anything goes'. However, this way of working invariably gives way to a more rigorous phase, a moment in the process that is often marked by a shift to a more hierarchical structure as a director takes the lead in sifting out what is inappropriate from the abundance of material that is generated in the first phase and bringing what remains into a coherent form. This process can seem brutal for the devisers, akin to the sort of directorial imposition suggested by Peter Brook (who, at the time of writing, was a few years down the line from *U.S.* (1966), his own experiment with collective devising): 'the director cuts away all that's extraneous, all that belongs just to the actor. ... You push and encourage the actor to discard all that is superfluous' (Brook, 1989, p. 4). However, in processes that maintain a collaborative or, in the case of Shunt, collective ethos, what the director aims for is 'consensus'. In an ideal situation, this is achieved when the group shares a vision – the views, values and organising principles that will determine the creative work. More usually, consensus is achieved through a director, the strength of whose vision encompasses or inspires those of individual group members. The more unified the group, the smoother the emergence of a coherent piece of theatre from the disparate elements that inspired it.

While the clash principle finds its purest form in the happening, the principle of consensus can be illustrated in the tradition of the ensemble which evolved when directors such as Meyerhold and Grotowski undertook serious explorations into theatre-making and performance. In order to develop practices that were distinct from the mainstream, these directors demanded 'a permanent group, breathing as one' and 'a single-minded commitment to company objectives' – this is the Maly Theatre Company under Lev Dodin described by Maria Shevtsova (2004, p. 34). The longevity and intensity of such groups turned them into a sort of family, invariably centred on the director as a charismatic patriarch (Ariane Mnouchkine and Joan Littlewood are rare exceptions to the male bias in this role). For such groups consensus is easy to achieve because the group shares the same values – and often also a willingness to submit to the director, as when one of Meyerhold's actors states that: 'he built a production as they built a house. And we were happy to be even a door-knob in this house' (quoted in Eyre and Wright, 2000, p. 349).

Although such hierarchy is alien to Shunt's policy of participatory equality and collective responsibility, the company does bear some of the hallmarks of an ensemble. For one thing, the company does have a director – though I will shortly argue that Rosenberg does not function in quite the same authorial way as those mentioned above. In keeping with the ensemble ethos, Shunt has a strong sense of its own independence from the established theatrical practices. Rosenberg states that 'we are a self-sufficient insular group which doesn't require anyone else.'[18] Although the *Lounge* has enabled the company to establish relationships with other like-minded practitioners, some of the artists tend to express a slightly scathing view of what they call 'theatre'. And their distinction from the mainstream is evident even before you see the work: the cultish feel of the website (featuring Dada-ist collages of packaging, signage, outdated advertising, faux Dymo-tape and stencilled lettering) and the process of negotiating what would normally be a box office – getting in to a Shunt show often include a long queue at the door in the hope that your name is on the list.

As with the ensemble, the Shunt artists share an aesthetic vision. The persistence with which they create an experiential encounter for the audience is evident from major decisions such as taking on disused spaces to use as performance venues, to the intricate details of their events. Jointly managing the company and the vast arts space in which they are based involves a lot of hard work and, given that the current funding situation cannot cover ten full-time salaries, some personal sacrifice. The members are willing to make this commitment because they share and believe in the company's principles. As Louise Mari says: 'everyone's heart is with Shunt.'[19]

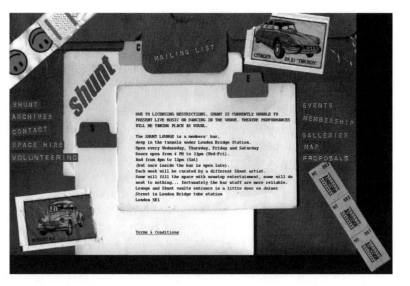

Figure 19   The Shunt website (designed by Pau Ros).

With this shared commitment to the company and its principles, Shunt demonstrates the prerequisites for creative agreement. The fact that this sits alongside the company's strong adherence to 'unfeasible' material determines the sort of work that they make. For successful devising depends to a great degree on finding the appropriate balance between clash and consensus. It is this balance that will determine how 'coherent' a performance will be and it is therefore an important indicator not just of the success of a production, but of the particular theatrical style that the company is establishing. The happening is a rare example of work that celebrates inconsistency and a lack of coherence. Such work might be usefully described as a 'collage', to adapt the term that David Graver (1995, pp. 31–40) uses to describe one of two constructive principles of avant-garde 'anti-art'. In the collage, the artwork is a framing device that holds together disparate found material: 'the fragments of reality are not fully integrated into the representational scheme of the work of art' (p. 31). More commonly, though, devised performance resembles what Graver describes as a 'montage', an artwork that brings together assorted material but forges it into a new whole so that 'all elements are related rationally to the whole despite the heterogeneity of their sources' (p. 31). Thus, even when a particular aesthetic style deliberately cultivates a fragmentary feel (as in the work of some devising companies), the resulting work is a coherent whole. And, generally speaking, the more coherent the performance, the more important it is for there to be consensus in the creative process. However, while agreement might seem a positive value (after all, it makes for a smoother process), too much may hinder the opportunity for innovation and novelty, and risk what the business world would call 'groupthink' – a too easy acceptance of any proposals made within a group to the point where non-conforming views are sidelined.

Shunt's work exemplifies this negotiation between clash and consensus, collage and montage. The Shunt *Cabaret* and the *Lounge* both clearly have a collage form, compartmenting the artists and encouraging parallel rather than interacting creative processes. This collage effect is also evident in the big shows which, as has been described earlier, are composed of a series of seemingly unrelated episodes in an odd assortment of locations (*Dance Bear Dance*, for example, starts with something like a meeting of UN delegates, includes a church service and a casino, and ends with something that is simultaneously the aftermath of a bomb-blast and a steam room and a curtain-call that is also a series of hangings conducted by a giant bear).

Incidentally, the big shows' disjointed narratives gives rise to the most common criticism of Shunt's work. *Tropicana*, for example, has been described as 'devoid of meaning, coherence or wit'.[20] The suggestion that the show lacked 'wit' is, I believe, just plain wrong. There are numerous moments that are humorous, poignant and undeniably witty: the disembodied high-heeled feet that patter around in the darkness (an illusion created quite simply by the performers pointing torches at their feet); Brockis' parodic accordion accompaniment to the mourners' hysterical outpourings of grief during the wake; the emergence of a be-feathered show-girl out of the corpse of a lift operator. My sense is that such reviews reflect a certain prejudice against experimental 'performance art', implied by the trepidation the reviewers describe at entering such unconventional territory. However, it is true that if the audience wants 'meaning', it needs to search quite hard for it. But this misses the point: the shows are experiential, driven by surprise, shock and an unsettling juxtaposition of different atmospheric environments rather than the revelation of 'meaning'.

Having said that, suggestions that a show is unfinished or 'uneven'[21] are justified to a degree – the shows do evolve in front of an audience over their extended runs and can take several weeks to really find their form. This just proves the point, however. My own experience of seeing *Amato Saltone* in its first week, with an unsatisfying and abrupt ending, revealed how carefully structured it later became. Although they retain a strategic fragmentation and 'incoherence', the Shunt shows are, in fact, coherent in their own terms, and strategically designed to create effective suspense, twists and well-timed climaxes. They are montages that retain the appearance of collages.

The collage effect of the big shows owes much to the 'show and tell' period of Shunt's devising process. This phase allows some agreement to be reached about general themes, source material and possible scenes, before the company moves on to the phase of building the sets, a task that involves all the artists. As space is obviously so integral to the shows, set-building is not only a necessary part of the process, but a creative one as well. In the case of *Tropicana*, the first show in the Vaults, the extensive work required to establish the infrastructure of the space meant that this phase of the process was particularly intense and, to some, frustrating:

> Lizzie [Clachan, the designer] and David were heavily involved at that point and Heather [Uprichard, performer] as well, who has a lot of building skills. Others helped out, but the performers didn't get into the set to start creating the show and to play until quite late on and that's something that really stressed them out.[22]

Incidentally, the fact that some artists felt more able than others to get involved with the building echoes the way in which the creative involvement of the artists is determined by their creative roles. Although the publicity material never credits the artists in particular roles (probably in order to avoid any impression of hierarchy), there are acknowledged areas of expertise and preference, often but not always coinciding with their training in a particular strand of the Advanced Theatre Practice Masters' course (which includes pathways in directing, performing, scenography, dramaturgy and writing for performance). There is a degree of flexibility in these roles, as Cooper suggests: 'There's room to step outside of their role. But Heather is a performer. Hannah, Gemma are performers but they all step outside of their roles. I would refer to it as their strength rather than their role.'[23]

This delicate negotiation between acknowledged roles which distinguish the artists and the collective ethos that allows them to offer opinions on any aspect of the performance-to-be is a reflection of the way in which clash and consensus are balanced in the company (even if there are points in the process for the big shows that are frustrating for some). Incidentally, this role definition can also in some instances limit individual artists' involvement in the *Lounge*. Uprichard, for example, commented that 'unless it's stand-up or live art, it's hard for a performer to just do work in the *Lounge*. I'm not interesting in doing solo work,' and that, therefore, for her the period of the *Lounge* has been 'been quite a frustrating and difficult couple of years'.[24]

Whatever the frustrations of individual artists, however, it is clear that from the point at which the sets are built, the process begins to demand expertise and distinct activities. In particular, it requires that Rosenberg steps forward in his role as director, 'creating the environment for improvisation and setting the right questions' so that the other members, often working in pairs or small sub-groups, can generate potential material.[25] The activity of showing potential work to the whole group remains important: it is the mechanism by which all the artists and collaborators contribute to the process. As scenes evolve through showings, feedback and re-working, Rosenberg's work is in 'trying to find the journey and how the many disparate elements can become coherent'. He is keen to stress that this journey is a collaborative one:

> Within a Shunt show, establishing that coherent journey is something that wouldn't be done just by me; it's something that would be done in conversation with other Shunt artists. ... The vision that I'm trying to implement is never my own, that vision came from a collective creation. Of course there are times when elements of hierarchy slip in, but usually it does feel that I am trying to implement the goal of the collective that has come out of rehearsal. Sure there're lots of fights but it's ok. It's always complicated but it's ok.[26]

The fact that this process is characterised as a struggle demonstrates that the company managed to retain an element of clash while trying to achieve consensus. The more distinct each individual Shunt artist remains within the group process, and the stronger they each are in expressing their views and contributing to that process, the more likely they are to retain a degree of exciting 'unfeasibility'. This is important for Shunt because, while the ensemble ethos is evidently a major factor in its success as an innovative and mould-breaking company, there is a concern that it may also create too much consensus:

> We have been working together for nearly ten years now and you start to get into that situation, when you are devising, if someone has an idea that they know doesn't kind of fit in with Shunty ideas, that they keep it to themselves or you start trying to think of things that you know are going to fit in with the group approach and so you get a kind of group sensibility. Everything gets smaller and smaller

and smaller and the ideas for it get smaller and smaller and smaller and the suggestions, in the same way, get more and more limited.[27]

The *Lounge* is a perfect mechanism for mitigating this. By separating the artists for an extended period of time and giving them the opportunity to take their work in new directions, it fosters the independence of vision of each of the Shunt artists. Whether or not any specific projects from the *Lounge* find their way into the forthcoming group event is beside the point. What the *Lounge* (and the *Cabaret* before it) allows the Shunt artists to do is evolve their individual visions, retaining their identities as separate artists. They do this through experimenting with the form and content of their work, but also through exploring different creative approaches, sometimes working outside their role. Twitchin, for example, who is usually the lighting designer, is currently creating, directing and occasionally performing. Rosenberg has been awarded a fellowship as an individual artist for the purpose of 'researching the environments, techniques and material that allow for an interactive, unique emotional experience [for the audience]',[28] particularly, as he said in interview, in terms of 'how work that is experiential for an audience could be written. Not as transcript of a performance but as a plan for performance.'[29] The more wholehearted and individual these explorations are, both in terms of subject matter and creative approach, the more the artists will have to 'bring to the table' once they come back together, in whatever form this might be. The *Lounge*, then, is an extended and brave example of the clash principle in action.

The clash principle encourages unorthodox conjunctions as separately created ideas, objects and performance segments eventually come together. It also allows for unexpected coincidences. I will end this chapter by describing one of these: the recurrence, in at least three of the projects emerging from the *Lounge*, of the image of the window. Windows seem to me to be an apt metaphor for the central principle of Shunt's work: the imperative to find new ways of negotiating the relationship between the audience and the performance, a new frame for the viewer and the object that is viewed. Having rejected the conventional theatrical set-up in which the place of performance is clearly defined by the existing architecture as separate from the audience, the Shunt artists continually create their own ways of framing, for the audience, that which 'has been composed for their perception'.[30]

Twitchin's 'frame pieces' use a wooden window frame (a found object) that is set on a pedestal on the stage area, abstracting the images within it from the architectural space in which the audience sits. In *In the Poorhouse*, the window frames a performer's hand which gestures and moves as an extract of Thomas Bernhard's *Breath* is read out. In *The Pianist* and *The Children's Emperor* the window holds a glass plate imprinted with a composite of black and white photographs. A torch is used to backlight different areas of the plates, directing the viewer's eye to the various scenes that resonate, in different ways, with the texts and music we hear. In Brockis and Mercuriali's *Pinocchio*, we are helpless passengers in a car driven by an impetuous and quarrelling twosome: the familiar city streets seem magically transformed through the windscreens and mirrors as we careen through them. Windows are also a key feature in *Contains Violence*. The works-in-progress at the *Lounge* used a set from *Amato Saltone* depicting a rooftop and two attic windows. The audience spies on the occupants of two lighted rooms as a commentary is fed through the earphones that have been provided. We learn that one of the people we are watching is an assassin (as she dons a wig) and we begin to suspect that the other will soon become her next victim. The final production, which took place from the terrace of the Lyric Hammersmith, used the existing windows of an office building across the main square from the theatre. Again, the performance uses the architectural form of the window to frame and compose the audience's perception, strategically revealing and hiding what we see (and what we know) in a way that is both humorous and highly suspenseful.

What this coincidence nicely exemplifies is the fact that, although the Shunt artists are clearly moving in new and different directions, there is actually a great deal of consensus between them. Despite a structure that deliberately compartments the artists, encouraging them to work in parallel rather than in collaboration, there are coincidental similarities in the work that has emerged from the *Lounge*. This, in turn, is a useful illustration of how a company might balance the conflicting desires for innovation and individual creative expression on one hand, and shared values and principles on the other. In other words, it demonstrates the way in which the *Lounge*, as in all Shunt's work, has achieved a cunning negotiation between clash and consensus.

Company members

The Shunt artists: Serena Bobowski, Gemma Brockis, Lizzie Clachan, Louise Mari, Hannah Ringham, Layla Rosa, David Rosenberg, Andrew Rutland, Mischa Twitchin, Heather Uprichard.
General Manager: Luke Cooper.
Building Manager: Andrea Salazar.

Chronology of productions

Twist (1998), for the Edinburgh Fringe Festival and Battersea Arts Centre's Octoberfest.

The Ballad of Bobby Francois (1999–2001), the Arch, the Pleasance for the 2000 Edinburgh Fringe Festival and Drome for the 2001 London International Mime Festival.

The Tennis Show (2001), The Museum of the Unknown, London.

Dance Bear Dance (2002–3), the Arch, London.

Tropicana (2004–5), the Vaults, London.

Amato Saltone Starring Kittens and Wade (2005–06), the Vaults, London.

Money (2009–10), 42–44 Bermondsey Street, London.

Performances by Shunt artists and associates cited in this chapter

These took place at the *Shunt Lounge* unless specified otherwise.

Twitchin, M.:

In the Poorhouse, 25–27 October 2006.

The Pianist, 25–27 October 2006, 16–19 January 2008.

The Children's Emperor, 16–19 January 2008.

Twitchin, M. and Tomlinson, G., *Laika in the Rust of Utopia*, 24–26 October and 31 October–2 November, 2007.

Ringham, H., *The Pigeon*, at the *Lounge* 10–13 October 2006 and 28 February–2 March 2007; at the Battersea Arts Centre, 2–4 February 2007.

Brockis, G. and Mercuriali, S., *Pinocchio*, at the Battersea Arts Centre 7–28 October 2006, 28 June–1 July 2007.

Rosa, L., *What If*, 6 October, 20 October and 3 November 2006.

Mari, L. and Barrett, N., *Mud Man*, numerous showings including 21–22 December 2006, 1–4 August 2007, 18–20 October 2007, 31 October–2 November 2007.

Rosenberg, D., *Contains Violence*, at the *Lounge* 6–8 September 2007, 10–13 October 2007 and 13 November 2007; at the Lyric Hammersmith, 26 April–10 May 2008.

Notes

1. Mischa Twitchin, interview with the author, 11 October 2007.
2. Susanne Dietz, '*Shunt Lounge*: A Musical Documentary about the *Shunt Lounge*, a Night-time Arts Space and Bar in the Vaults under London Bridge Station' (posted on YouTube 27 February 2008). Available at http://uk.youtube.com/watch?v=KJSQlIBgCOw (accessed 30 April 2008).
3. Twitchin, interview with the author, 11 October 2007.
4. For images see Van der Crabben, J. 'Shunt 2007', set of personal photographs from the *Shunt Lounge*. Available at http://www.flickr.com/photos/jvdc/sets/72157600149040445/ (accessed 30 April 2008).
5. Louise Mari, interview with the author, 9 November 2006.
6. Twitchin, M., Presentation at the 'Low-down' Symposium on Collaboration at Camden People's Theatre, 6 April 2002.

7. Heather Uprichard, quoted in Colville, R., *The Observer*, 21 March 2004.
8. David Rosenberg, interview with the author, 10 December 2007.
9. Katy Guest, '101 Star Bars', 1 September 2007. Available at www.independent. co.uk/life-style/food-and-drink/reviews/101-star-bars-25-shunt-lounge-london-463448.html (accessed 25 March 2008).
10. Rose Day, C., Review of the *Shunt Lounge* on Fluid Foundation. Date not given (probably May 2007). Available at www.fluidfoundation.com/venue-details.aspx?VenueID=19208 (accessed 25 March 2008).
11. The Shunt website (no author/date given). Available at www.shunt.co.uk (accessed 27 April 2008).
12. Rosenberg, interview with the author, 10 December 2007.
13. Luke Cooper, interview with the author, 3 December 2007.
14. Gemma Brockis, presentation at the Creative Producing symposium at the Museum of the unknown, 23 October 2000, p. 8.
15. Mari, interview with the author, 9 November 2006.
16. Cooper, interview with the author, 3 December 2007.
17. Layla Rosa (nee Marlin), interview with the author, 30 November 2006.
18. Rosenberg, interview with the author, 10 December 2007.
19. Mari, interview with the author, 9 November 2006.
20. Nicholas De Jonge, 'Theatre Down the Tube' (review of *Tropicana*), *Evening Standard*, 25 October 2004.
21. For example see Kellaway, K., 'Going Underground' (review of *Tropicana*), *The Observer*, 25 October 2004.
22. Cooper, interview with the author, 3 December 2007.
23. Ibid.
24. Uprichard, interview with the author, 3 December 2007.
25. Rosenberg, interview with the author, 10 December 2007.
26. Ibid.
27. Mari, interview with the author, 9 November 2006.
28. NESTA (National Endowment for Science, Technology and the Arts), 'Awardee and Recipient Archive: David Rosenberg', on the Nesta website, available at www.nesta.org.uk/david-rosenberg (accessed April 2008).
29. Rosenberg, interview with the author, 10 December 2007.
30. Twitchin, interview with the author, 3 December 2007.

8

Sculpting the Territory

Gecko's *The Arab and The Jew* in Process

Jackie Smart

Beginnings

Gecko was formed in 2001 by co-artistic directors Amit Lahav and Allel Nedjari, with technical director Stuart Heyes (although Heyes later stood down). The company aims for their work to 'serve as a launch pad for our audiences' imaginations, awakening their senses and engaging their emotions'; they describe their style as involving 'great athleticism and emotional expressiveness.'[1] *The Arab and The Jew* is Gecko's third production. The previous two shows, *Taylor's Dummies* (2002) and *The Race* (2005), toured nationally and internationally, garnering a number of awards including a Total Theatre award for *The Race*, *Time Out* Critics' Choice and Live Awards for *Taylor's Dummies*, and *Guardian* Pick of the Fringe awards for both these shows. These productions were each highly physical, developed around themes personal to the participants and imbued with clown-like humour. Gecko uses little speech in its work, the structure of which resembles a collage of images and actions that are often multi-layered in their significance. There is a sense of story in its pieces but the company does not deal in narrative chains of cause and effect so much as journeys of emotional understanding; the structural signposts Gecko employs tend to be visual, physical and musical rather than verbal, so its shows are less pre-determined and more open to audience interpretation than a conventional linear narrative.

Taylor's Dummies received enthusiastic critical feedback from the outset: the *London Evening Standard* praised its 'panache and dark wit ... its exuberance, its sensual physicality and its ability to play dizzyingly with perspective'.[2] In the later stages of its development, *The Race* too was critically acclaimed but it is interesting to note that responses changed as the show developed. *Guardian* critic Lyn Gardner was disappointed when she first saw *The Race* in February 2005 at BAC, comparing it unfavourably with *Taylor's Dummies*. She wrote:

> [*Taylor's Dummies*] was one of those unexpected surprises that make being a critic such a pleasure. Here was a physical theatre company doing a debut that was assured, witty, thoughtful and quite astonishing in the way it used every inch of space to tell its story of misplaced and thwarted love. Now ... Gecko graduate to BAC's main space and, alas, fall flat on their faces. Not literally, of course – they are far too accomplished as physical performers for that. But just as the second play is always difficult for the traditional playwright, it proves to be just as hard a nut to crack in the physical theatre world.'3

By the time of its Edinburgh Fringe production though, Gardner had revised her opinion and *The Race* became the *Guardian*'s Pick of the Fringe. As this chapter will reveal, Gecko productions are in continual development and early versions of a show can be very different from later ones.

Gecko's work is characterised as physical theatre by Lahav and Nedjari themselves and by others, but this label does not tell the whole story; the range of styles and skills on which the company draws is multiple and eclectic, embracing elements of mime and clowning, dance, circus and more conventional character-based theatre. Design and music are also extremely important to them. Nedjari and Lahav have long experience as performers and it is very much *as* performers that they create their work, a facet of their process on which I focus in this chapter. In *The Arab and The Jew*, the company has also taken tentative steps towards a form of political theatre. Lahav and Nedjari would certainly not claim to be primarily concerned with the political impact of the piece; however, during the process of its making they became increasingly willing to consider it in socio-political terms. This has been a fascinating aspect of the journey they have taken and it is one to which I will pay special attention.

Alongside their production work, Gecko has a strong commitment to participatory activities. Their interest in this was sparked by their involvement in the David Glass Ensemble's *Lost Child Project*, 'an international project for empowering the creativity of marginalised young people' (Glass, 2003, p. vi). Gecko writes that 'the principles of participatory work are inherent in the company's own methodology.'4 Lahav and Nedjari's experience within the David Glass Ensemble has been important to them in other ways too. Glass trained with Jacques Lecoq, as did

Steven Berkoff, with whom both Lahav and Nedjari have also worked. This mutual experience of a Lecoq-influenced physical training gives them a shared methodological vocabulary on which to draw.

Lecoq's influence is usually described more in terms of his system of teaching than of any defined method. In his book *Le Corps Poetique* (The Moving Body), he explains that his students follow two parallel paths, the first being a 'study of improvisation and its rules' and the second a 'study of movement technique and its analysis' (Lecoq, 2001, p. 14). Both playful, improvisatory exploration and physical openness and skill feature prominently in Gecko's approach. More importantly, the concept of the 'actor as creator' (Chamberlain and Yarrow, 2002, p. 9) which lies at the heart of Lecoq's educational philosophy is central to Gecko's process. Nedjari and Lahav's love of clowning is also in part traceable to Lecoq. The humour of Lecoq's clown is based around the individual exposing 'naiveté' and 'fragility' (Lecoq, 2001, p. 145), qualities essential to the characterisation of Nedjari's 'Arab' and Lahav's 'Jew'.

Gecko differs from the David Glass Ensemble and other Lecoq-influenced companies such as Complicite and theatre O, however, in that they have not, so far, used an existing story or text as a starting point.[5] Instead, their main sources of subject matter have been their own experiences, relationships and emotional responses to the world. This is an approach more common to dance-based physical theatre companies such as DV8 or Ultima Vez and, as in these companies, the characters created by Lahav and Nedjari emerge from and represent various aspects of their own personalities. The worlds they create on stage are representative of inner states or dream worlds, reminiscent of those created by Pina Bausch and Jan Fabre.

Lahav and Nedjari themselves assert that one of the strongest influences on their working method is their own cultural heritage. As they explain in the programme for a work-in-progress performance, this factor was a starting point for *The Arab and The Jew*.

> During the development of our working relationship it has dawned on us that our respective 'Arabness' and 'Jewishness' may indeed be [an] essential ingredient [of] the way we operate. ... We share a certain exuberance and otherness with which we express ourselves and communicate artistically; a direct influence from our parents, grandparents and relatives and our experiences. At the same time, we too have our Arab and Israeli flags buried somewhere deep within us. And so, when the issue of Arabs and Israel is raised, as

so often happens, due to the barrage of images and stories we see and hear, we engage in a careful dance of reason and conciliation, our deep-rooted unconscious allegiances simmering beneath the surface.[6]

This aspect of Gecko's identity has resonances with another strand of contemporary devising practice. Govan, Nicholson and Normington point out the frequency with which 'metaphors of place and space – borders, margins, mappings, translocation, dislocation and so on' are used to explore concepts of individual and social identity in our globalised, mobile world (2007, p. 136). They discuss such metaphors in relation to site-specific and community theatre, where they often express the experience of multiple or divided identity people of mixed ethnic or cultural heritage can feel. In *The Arab and The Jew*, Lahav and Nedjari undertake a highly personal investigation into their own ethnic and cultural heritage and how that affects their relationship. Although they have frequently excavated interior emotional material for creative use, cultural difference was an area they approached with some apprehension. They were, after all, making their personal relationship – including its previously unspoken conflicts – the subject of private and public scrutiny, albeit in 'fictional' form.

Before I look in detail at the creative process of *The Arab and The Jew*, it is important to take into consideration some of the practical and economic matters which affect any medium-scale touring company, as these can shape process and outcome in significant ways. The table below shows key staging posts of the creation of *The Arab and The Jew*. Nedjari and Lahav's thinking and discussion about the show began long before January 2007 and, as is often the case with devised work, the company never considers any production to be finally finished, so as they continue to tour it internationally it continues to develop. My observation took place from January 2007 to January 2008. Of course I was not present in every rehearsal but the extraordinary openness and creative generosity of Lahav and Nedjari meant that I was able to sit in frequently. I saw most work-in-progress presentations and saw performances in Bristol, Edinburgh, Watford and London.

The Arab and The Jew was co-commissioned by the Drum Theatre in Plymouth, the Lyric Theatre in Hammersmith, London, the New Wolsey theatre in Ipswich and the Tobacco Factory in Bristol. 'In-kind' support – which usually consists of the provision of rehearsal space and resources rather than actual cash – was provided by a further four theatres: the Corn Exchange in Newbury, the Junction in Cambridge,

January 2007: Rehearsals begin.

February: Half-term residency with schoolchildren in Poole.

Late March: First work-in-progress performances, New Wolsey Theatre, Ipswich.

Early June: WIP Performances: New Greenham Arts, Newbury; the Junction, Cambridge.

28 June: Confirmation of Arts Council grant.

Early August: Pre-Edinburgh run, Tobacco Factory, Bristol.

August: Performances, British Council Showcase, Edinburgh.

Sept–Dec: Tour: Bracknell; Luton; St Albans; Cambridge; Warwick; Watford; Ipswich; Worthing.

18 Jan–9 Feb 2008: Performances, London International Mime Festival, Lyric Theatre, Hammersmith.

9 Feb onwards: Further national and international tours.

Figure 20   Rehearsal and performance schedule for *The Arab and The Jew*.

South Hill Park in Bracknell and Warwick Arts Centre. Venues such as these offer their support on the basis that companies undertake audience-development activities during the process of creating a piece: these include workshops, residencies and work-in-progress performances. Companies then usually return to the venue with the 'finished' production. I discuss the implications and consequences of this system in more depth later, but something to highlight here is that it means Gecko were presenting publicly sections and versions of *The Arab and The Jew* from the very early stages of its development. It also meant that they were moving around the country between different rehearsal spaces. This is not an unusual situation for a small-scale touring company but it does have an impact on how shows progress and develop. It means the creative period can be quite fragmented and the company has to be flexible in terms of space.

Another factor in the development of the show was the fact that the company was asked to re-submit its application for Arts Council funding and did not receive final confirmation of this project-based funding until 28 June 2007. This financial uncertainty meant that Gecko was unable to guarantee payment for a permanent design and technical team, with the consequence that Lahav and Nedjari relied for the first seven months on a revolving group of loyal friends and supporters to help them explore the design aspects of the show and construct set and props. For example, Lahav had been very keen to work with the artist Dryden Goodwin, and Goodwin did spend three very productive days with the company in the early stages when they were playing with initial ideas but, as Gecko were unable to guarantee payment for an extended period, he could not stay on as a creative collaborator. A further result of the delay in funding was that a great deal of time and energy was expended on the re-application process and on other fundraising activities. Although this is clearly stressful and frustrating, it is a common experience of many companies and points to the degree of resilience and faith in their creative ideas that such practitioners must have if they are to succeed in producing a show.

Quotations from the company in the following sections of this chapter are from informal conversations I had with Lahav and Nedjari during breaks in rehearsals unless otherwise indicated.

The process

David Glass has produced an 'ideal' methodology for creative development (Glass, 2003). Although focused around participatory work rather than the creation of a professional theatre performance, given Lahav and Nedjari's familiarity with this methodology, it serves as an instructive point of comparison with their own creative process. This is a comparison I have chosen to make rather than one which was suggested by Gecko, who emphasise that their experience with the David Glass Ensemble has been one influence among many in their development as actors and as a company.

Glass presents his methodology in five stages:

1. **Preparation** focuses on: creating a safe and productive environment; preparing the bodies and minds of individuals through training and exercises; encouraging openness and receptivity in the relationships between company members.
2. **Creative origination** is where ideas for a piece are elicited and generated, explored and developed in practice.
3. **Creative organisation** is about focus and structure: it draws ideas together and develops the overall meaning of a project.

4. **Manifestation/presentation** is the performance of the creative project.
5. **Reflection and renewal** enables participants to consider critically what they have achieved, receive feedback and set new goals for future development.

Glass emphasises the importance of 'creative cycling' (2003, p. 9) meaning that, rather than thinking of process as a one-way journey towards a single goal, one should envision it as moving back and forth through the stages, perhaps resulting in numerous different 'manifestations'. My observation of Gecko showed me that different stages can also occur simultaneously. In fact, the process of creating *The Arab and The Jew* was surprisingly fluid and cyclic.

Preparation

I concentrate on two interconnected aspects of preparation in this section: the first concerns training and the development of the physical 'vocabulary' of the show; the second has to do with its subject matter and the research connected with this. Starting with research, in the first rehearsal I observed, three days into Gecko's first formal week of active development, I asked Lahav and Nedjari what they intended the show to be about. They told me that the notion of a show about Arabs and Jews had had a long gestation period, having entered their heads when they were working on *The Race* (2005), but that they already felt they were departing from that and moving more towards the subject of 'brotherhood'. They wanted, they said, to explore their 'theatrical relationship'. There was no intention to create an overtly political piece and they did not undertake any specific research into either the current situation in the Middle East or its historical genesis. Many months later, when I reminded Nedjari of this initial definition of their subject matter, he responded:

> What has been the journey of the show is the unfolding realisation that actually this is a political show and we want to make a political point and we didn't admit it to ourselves when we first started, even though we were turned on by calling it *The Arab and The Jew*. ... We hid behind the cloak of 'this is going to be a show which is about Amit and I and our relationship.'[7]

This reveals that the process of making the show was, in itself, a piece of emotional research, a way of accessing feelings and attitudes which lay below the level of consciousness, and creating a safe environment in which to explore them imaginatively. Even for such experienced performers as Nedjari and Lahav who know each other well and have worked together over a long period, it took time to get to the stage where they were able to see clearly and discuss openly what they were aiming towards. This was potentially an emotionally dangerous journey on which to embark; Lahav and Nedjari told themselves at the beginning that they were exploring what they felt they shared, but they would also be exploring how they differed, bringing into the light some areas of conflict which had previously remained unspoken. The oblique approach the pair initially took to their subject matter was a way of building themselves up emotionally to the point where they were comfortable enough to face it more directly. Talking to me some months after the Lyric run, Lahav emphasised how important he felt it was *not* to know everything a show might be about at the beginning of the process as, he felt, this could close down essential aspects of the creative exploration. 'Not knowing' is something Gecko celebrate.[8]

In terms of physical preparation, Lahav and Nedjari start with a shared vocabulary born of the similar trajectories of their previous experience, and of course they had already made two productions together. Nevertheless, they needed to discover and become fluent in the particular 'language' of this project. They undertook lengthy and demanding warm-ups which, as well as developing their strength, stamina and flexibility, honed their ability to communicate with and respond to one another physically. The remarkable levels of physical understanding between these two performers on stage are testament to the attention they pay to this aspect of preparation.

They also undertook some specialist training in the art of boxing. They knew from a very early stage that they wanted a boxing match in the piece so this was a practical necessity, but it was also a very important way of working through some of the feelings and responses they wanted to explore. Lahav told me about a moment during this boxing training where Nedjari 'caught me and I reacted to being caught. ... I think it was clear to both of us that I reacted. Rather than just being in the moment, I said, "Right, you hit me, I'm going to hit you back now."'[9] Lahav acknowledged that he had frightened himself with his own sense of aggression but emphasised that this kind of emotional discovery was essential to their journey. It is in this sense that the two aspects of preparation I have addressed are linked. The body is not disconnected from the mind or the emotions: through physical experiment Gecko

Figure 21   Gecko in rehearsal in Bristol, July 2007. Photo by Jackie Smart.

opens up mental and emotional lines of exploration. Reflecting on this stage of process after the Lyric run, Lahav said:

> It's impossible to separate the subjects: to say, 'it's about brotherhood but it's not about territory; it's about territory but it's not about war; it's about people but it's not about conflict.' It is, it is – you touch it, you touch the conflict, you touch the problem – it just reaches into all areas.[10]

Creative origination

In the David Glass model this stage is a time to ask questions and explore, to open up the potential scope of a project before organising it into any fixed narrative, structure or meaning. Nedjari and Lahav approach this process from a number of different directions, playing with images, actions, pieces of music, objects and environments. They also talk a great deal; going for a coffee was a surprisingly important part of the origination process of *The Arab and The Jew*, often helping them to free up a tangle of ideas or overcome a block. The relaxed, social dynamic of a café suited their personalities and produced free-flowing, stream-of-consciousness exchanges, full of visual and sound-based images, many of which would seem to be forgotten but would then reappear, sometimes months later, in the show.

Several ideas had been 'hanging around' since well before formal rehearsals began – for instance, a notion that they would play a pair of performers. When my observation began they were playing with the idea that they would be trombonists in an orchestra and were searching for a piece of music which would create 'the right rhythm of occurrences between us', allowing for both harmony and the sense of a hidden conflict or competition. They never found the right music for this though; instead they settled on a version of *You Always Hurt the One You Love* which had 'been around for a while, even pre *Arab and Jew*, [as a] piece of music that we wanted to put a routine to'.[11] Similarly, they had been toying with the idea of having 'a real fight' in the show for a long time. These two initial ideas encapsulate the thematic heart of *The Arab and The Jew*: Lahav and Nedjari simultaneously celebrating their relationship as performers and interrogating the hidden conflicts within it. Another stream feeding into the initial flow of ideas came directly from their respective family heritages:

> [the old men in the café] is an image of our fathers, both of whom are overweight, overbearing Middle Eastern guys, and quite clown-like. ... I definitely think that one of the starting points for the show was giving them a voice and a vehicle.[12]

Physical improvisation was a key strategy for creating actions and developing them into sequences. When working physically, Lahav and Nedjari tended not to spend a long time on any one thing but to shift between several different ideas: developing each incrementally, filming everything and frequently breaking off to watch themselves and discuss what they saw and how they felt about it. Some ideas grew out of classic physical exercises. For example, one physical routine (which later acquired the shorthand title 'status-gripping') was a sequence in which an initial handshake of greeting between two friends develops into increasingly aggressive and competitive movement, the physical principle being that contact should be maintained throughout. Other improvisations were derived from images, one from something they had seen on YouTube. In this improvisation, one played a horse and the other a trainer trying to 'break him in' and get a rope around him. They tried this first with Lahav 'breaking' Nedjari and then the other way around, again filming it and watching it back, discussing how it felt to each of them in the different roles. To me, observing, both these ideas were clearly concerned with notions of power, status and control, playing with the levels of hostility that can exist between friends. Lahav and Nedjari, though, were not particularly interested in in-depth discussion of the meanings behind what they were doing while they were doing it; Lahav explained that, at this stage, they felt that 'intellectualising' would close down what it was they were trying to reach.

I later came to understand this resistance to fixing meaning from a different perspective, connected to Lahav's and Nedjari's personal explorations of their own cultural identities. In parallel to the activities described above, the two were developing ideas about personal journeys that each would take into his own cultural heritage. This was to be expressed spatially in terms of 'rooms', separate areas of the stage to which each would travel and in which they would 'discover' their respective 'Israeliness' and 'Arabness'. The development of these individual 'rooms' was, necessarily, a personal rather than a joint activity and proved to be a creatively thorny area. Looking back on this aspect of the process in October 2007 Lahav and Nedjari talked of the different relationship each has with his cultural experience. Lahav said:

> I was able to attach myself to images and metaphors quite quickly ... and say 'ah, it's about family, celebration and hands and people and gestures and gifts.' ... It's been much more difficult for Al ... he's been searching and that's painful for him.[13]

Explaining that he was mainly brought up in England by an English mother, Nedjari said:

> I have a distant and romantic connection with my Arabness and Amit has a closer, more immediate relationship to his Israeliness, which is why I think his area developed so much more readily than ... mine.[14]

In fact it was not until after the Edinburgh run of the show, eight months into the project, that Nedjari really began to develop his 'room' beyond what he himself called 'a sort of stereotypical, almost frivolous, image of Arabness.'[15] This highlights an important point about creative origination. For Gecko, this stage is never over; new ideas, or changes in the direction of existing ideas, kept emerging throughout the process as the performers attained various stages of emotional readiness. When you are dealing with personal material, no matter how much you want to explore certain areas, there can be a kind of inner reluctance which is hard to overcome and resistant to pressure. Lahav stressed the creative importance of 'time out': 'sometimes, when I actively stop mentally searching, I am gifted with the very idea or image I was searching for.'[16] Another reason for time out, when you are a two-man outfit, is to create a little space between you, especially when the subject matter is your-selves and your relationship. This was quite a fragmented process with many breaks, mainly necessitated by other work commitments. Often, when I saw Gecko after such a break, a veritable flood of ideas seemed to have built up, ready to pour forth.

Creative organisation

In this stage of process, the focus in David Glass's model is 'on the creation of connections, relationships, priorities, structures and mean-ing'. Glass emphasises the symbiotic relationship between Origination and Organisation, stating that 'we can think of [them] as two sides of one stage that acts as the centre of creative practice' (2003, p. 76). In *The Arab and The Jew*, Origination and Organisation were like two ends of a seesaw, with the balance of activity shifting back and forth between them throughout the process. Part of the reason for this is that the process as a whole was punctuated by presentations of work in progress. Hence, while Gecko was still generating ideas, it was also organising them into performable 'chunks'. This means that the final two stages of Glass's model, Manifestation and Reflection, were also occurring concurrently, because the company was presenting work to public audiences and receiving feedback upon it.

Work-in-progress performances (WIPs) are used much more in devised practice than in other forms of theatre and grew out of its col-laborative nature and its emphasis on process over product. However, it can be venues, rather than the company, which control when a WIP will take place, and there were times during my observation of *The Arab and The Jew* when I felt that Gecko was having to rehearse in public in the sense that they were presenting work while it was still at quite a raw and tender stage. Given the personal nature of their explo-ration, I wondered how they felt about this. Nedjari felt the system was 'intrinsic' to their practice:

> It is ... an absolutely instrumental thing in the piecing together of the show because ... in a real true sense of the word we're performers; we

deal with a live audience, and you can only deal with a live audience by being in front of a live audience so a lot of the parameters of the show that we need to grapple with we only learn about by doing it in front of an audience.[17]

Lahav also acknowledged the positive functions of WIPs, saying they were a useful 'galvanising factor … a way to make things move on incredibly quickly and to make enormous discoveries'. He also felt, though, that:

It can be both literally, physically dangerous, and emotionally heavy and stressful. … You have to look people in the face who are not on your journey and I find that hard. It takes some nerve and confidence to be reaching into the distance whilst in no way appearing defensive or apologetic to a new audience.[18]

These responses illustrate a tension between the sharing of their creative process as an essential and defining factor of the way they work and the stresses this brings with it.

The WIPs in Ipswich in March and Newbury in early June illustrate different stages and methods of organisational work. Gecko's attitude towards their first WIP at the New Wolsey Theatre in Ipswich was that it was 'an initial foray, just sticking a flag in the sand'. A fortnight before the WIP they had a number of images and interactions they had been playing with, but no pre-determined order and no fully worked-out overall 'meaning'. Lahav and Nedjari both keep books in which they record aspects of process and note down ideas. Each had a list of potential 'scenes' defined by shorthand titles (see Figure 22). Some of these were scenes they had worked on, some were ideas they had talked through, some were ideas they liked but had not developed at all. Listening to them debate which of these they might show and what order they might put them in, I realised that this was an exercise in clarifying for themselves what their show was about; meaning and structure were being actively negotiated between them as the conversation went on. It was interesting to see that scenes and images did not necessarily mean the same thing to each of them. Frequently, one would describe a scene as he saw it, then the other would say 'or they …' and go on to offer a different perspective. They were relaxed about these differences of opinion and, surprisingly, whether or not they had developed or worked on an idea was not necessarily a criterion for inclusion.

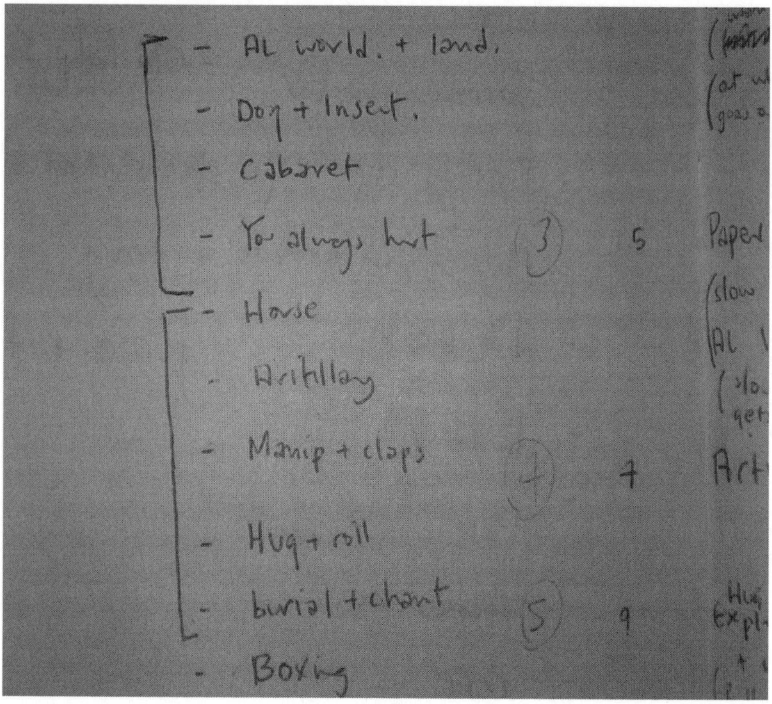

Figure 22 Amit Lahav's notebook showing a list of potential scenes for *The Arab and The Jew*, December 2007. Photo by Jackie Smart.

The fact that the Ipswich audience were aware that this was a first-stage presentation lifted the pressure and enabled Gecko to treat it as a genuine exploration, so they were willing to take risks on relatively undeveloped material so long as they found it interesting conceptually. In contrast, when I caught up with them again a couple of days before the WIP, I found them ensconced in a café with earphones and laptop, paying forensic attention to the creation of a sound score for the presentation. Lahav has 'always been a collector of music',[19] and music and sound play an extremely important part both in inspiring ideas and in structuring the journey through Gecko's shows. For the Ipswich WIP the musical score was used to give a rhythmic shape to the collection of scenes they had decided on; it functioned almost like a script, offering a defined framework and set of timings within which they would, to a greater or lesser degree, improvise around ideas.

This WIP moved the show from existing as a collection of images and ideas to having a basically worked-out structure. In part this came from the music but a second important aspect of development refers us back to Nedjari's statement about their definition of themselves as performers. Essentially, it is in performance that he and Lahav are most able to clearly hear and see what has been fermenting in their minds and imaginations. The concrete job of guiding the audience through the emotional journey of a moment and from moment to moment, as actors, illuminates the journey they are involved in. Lahav says:

> The world of the show comes into focus, not intellectually, but internally. The landscape somehow locks into my body and I physically understand the boundaries of this theatrical world. ... The appropriateness of ideas becomes more obvious.[20]

Leading up to the Newbury WIP, Gecko had one week's rehearsal in the space, and for the first time they had Stuart Heyes, their production manager, with them. With access to technicians and technical resources previously unavailable, their focus in Newbury was to experiment with set design. The result was to provoke a whole new phase of creative development. The set they built in Newbury (which they constructed largely from whatever materials they could find at the venue) was based upon an early concept of a white-walled, 'neutral' location into which their two characters would fall at the beginning of the piece. These characters would not know where or who they were; it would be through their journeys into their individual 'rooms' that they would rediscover their respective cultural identities and, bringing these back into the neutral space, they would re-enact the conflicted relationships of their past to the point where they would both 'die' in an explosion in a café. The white space, therefore, was representative of an otherworldly, meeting place within which the journey of their 'lived' relationship could be re-viewed on a symbolic plane.

The opportunity to perform within this set in Newbury, however, awakened in them a sense of the significance of the space itself and their characters' struggle for possession of it, causing an important shift of focus from their relationship with each other to their relationship with the land. I believe it was this realisation that provoked them to start thinking more overtly of their piece as 'political theatre' because it illuminated the fact that the area of hidden conflict between them was *not* solely personal, but grew out of a territory which was contested in both geographical and historical terms.

This led to an interesting situation. *The Arab And The Jew* was booked to run at the Edinburgh Fringe and for preview performances in Bristol beforehand. The Newbury WIP had opened up exciting new potential for the show. Nedjari and Lahav returned to central questions about meaning, character and structure, exploring them on a more sophisticated level through interrogating the relationship between the 'internal' territory of their characters' conflicted brotherhood and its roots in the 'external' territory of the land. However, because of work and family commitments, they did not feel they had sufficient time both to fully explore these new areas and to fix and polish to the necessary standard. So they focused on creating a coherent production for Edinburgh, knowing that what they would present there would only be a stage in the show's development. I wondered if this would be problematic but Gecko saw it as an opportunity to gain depth through doing a run of performances. Nedjari explains:

> What Edinburgh enabled us to do was to say: 'Here's a stage of development, a milestone in the show's development. Let's wring it for all its worth in terms of how we now perform this and learn what we can about the individual scenes and about how this, as a structure for the future, works.'[21]

The other important aspect of the Bristol and Edinburgh runs was that the long-awaited confirmation of Arts Council funding allowed Gecko to employ lighting designer Jackie Shemesh. Lahav's partner, Helen Baggett (herself a dancer and choreographer), operates as an informal outside eye for Gecko. She had seen various runs and offered respected commentary and advice. Jackie, though, had not been privy, as Baggett had, to the gradual development of ideas, so when he saw a run, it was a fresh experience for him. He also watched from a different viewpoint: he is Israeli and has lived in Tel Aviv so the political element of the show had particular resonances for him.

It was fascinating to hear him talk through the run as he saw and understood it, suggesting ideas for lighting effects as he went along. While watching he had done a series of sketches of the different positions of the actors at various points, which he used to offer a kind of spatial narrative. This led to his suggestion of breaking up the stage into 'key areas' through lighting to help guide the audience along the characters' emotional journeys as they explored and rediscovered their respective cultural heritages. For example, early in the show a doll representing the 'Jew's' child seems to guide Lahav's character in a particular direction. Shemesh suggested a sharply defined corridor of light at the front of the stage in order to emphasise the sense of a journey to another world. Sometimes his vision of the lighting for a scene gave its meaning an added dimension. For instance, the idea of a fluorescent white strip light for the boxing match would bring out the stark brutality of the real Israel–Palestine conflict, operating in contrast to the colourful and dreamlike atmosphere of the rest of the piece. In this way, Shemesh's narrative of space and light helped add a new layer of politically and culturally informed meaning to the Edinburgh production.

Manifestation/presentation

For David Glass a defining characteristic of this stage is the shifting of focus from 'inward' to 'outward' (Glass, 2003, p. 77), from the performers' private journey of exploration to their encounter with an audience. As we have already seen, for Gecko encounters with audiences occurred throughout their process, playing a pivotal role in the creative development of the show. The Edinburgh version of *The Arab and The Jew* was one version of a show which Gecko then took in a new direction for their January 2008 run at London's Lyric Theatre, Hammersmith. In a conversation with *Guardian* theatre critic Lyn Gardner, Lahav and Nedjari explained that the Edinburgh run had reinforced for them how sensitive their material was:

> Some audience members were unhappy that the Jewish character floated gently to the ground, while the Arab fell with a plop. For some, this lack of grace reinforced negative Arab stereotypes. 'People were actually arguing over who should land first, too,' says Lahav. 'For them it was an incredibly important statement, because it got to the nub of their beliefs about who was on that land first and therefore who had the greater claim to it.'[22]

It would be incorrect to imply that Gecko started trying to offer a defined political message; it did not. The production remained abstract in style, the meanings of individual images and actions always open to interpretation and the overall emotional effect coming out of the accumulation of associative ideas rather than from a linear narrative. Reviewers understood this. *Guardian* critic Brian Logan wrote that the show 'bypasses politics, illuminating the Arab–Israeli relationship as scorched fragments in a sometimes ravishing display of theatrical fireworks,'[23] while another review stated: '*The Arab and The Jew* focuses on people rather than politics, layering image upon image, to create a picture of a world full of connections and divisions.'[24]

Nedjari and Lahav did accept though that a show called *The Arab and The Jew* was always going to carry associations with the situation in Israel/Palestine, and their confidence in being overtly political grew throughout the process. At the Lyric, the issue of the relationship between the territory 'within' and the territory 'without' became much more prominent. For example, the individual journeys taken by the 'Arab' and the 'Jew' were now more directly related to suggestions of a concrete place. The central area, which had originally been conceived of as a neutral space, was now covered in sand. In one very powerful and beautiful image, Lahav and Nedjari sculpted this sand into a series of hills and valleys, mountains and lakes, which suggested an actual land, precious to them both. The differences between the attitudes of the two characters to this land were now also more clearly signalled. As the 'Arab', Nedjari descended through the sandy stage into his 'room', within which the voice of his father was heard speaking in Arabic and in English, describing how 'orange trees grew over the house [in] your land.' In contrast, Lahav, as the 'Jew', climbed upwards into his 'room', where he was given a small glowing light, a 'seed', which he then buried in the sand of the stage. Brian Logan interpreted these images as contrasting 'the Arab's sensual, familial bond to the land with the Jew's sense of spiritual entitlement'.[25] Lahav and Nedjari refuse to comment on their own sense of what the show as a whole or particular images within it might mean, insisting that any individual interpretation is valid.

Some images that had emerged very early remained in the show throughout all its stages. One of these was the 'horse training' sequence (with the 'Jew' training the 'Arab'); another was the boxing match. The continual presence of such images in the production takes me back to the very early stages of my observation, when Lahav and Nedjari told me they were making a piece about 'brotherhood'. Beneath the conflicts in the show, the 'brotherhood' between the characters remained powerfully present, not least because of the remarkable levels of theatrical communication and trust demonstrated by Lahav and Nedjari as performers. It was the strength of the working bond between these two artists which allowed them to explore the conflicts within it and which, for me, gave the production its power and sense of truth.

Reflection and renewal

As I have shown, reflection and renewal occur on a continuous basis throughout Gecko's process. Thus I feel justified in hijacking this final stage for my own overall reflection on my observation of the creation of *The Arab and The Jew* and drawing out what I consider to be key aspects of Gecko's devising process.

Lahav and Nedjari's shared physical and cultural language is an essential starting point but Gecko is not a company which operates within any particular methodology. 'Surprising' and 'unexpected' are words that crop up frequently in descriptions or reviews of Gecko performances, and this is because their modus operandi is eclecticism. The language of the show grows out of the demands of the exploration rather than any pre-existing system or approach, while their process is fluid and cyclical. Lahav and Nedjari are immensely positive by nature and this has proven to be a great strength in their ability to cope with the many practical difficulties with which the system of arts funding presents them. In the current economic climate, the relationship between companies like Gecko and small to mid-scale venues is both hugely important and mutually beneficial: venues provide much-needed practical support and help the company to develop their show through work-in-progress performances; the company helps venues build and develop their audience.

While Gecko employs a range of strategies for provoking and encouraging creativity, it is also true to say that an idea takes its own time to emerge fully. This process was a genuine exploration, and a brave one,

Figure 23   Gecko in rehearsal in Bristol, July 2007. Photo by Jackie Smart.

in which Lahav and Nedjari were willing to expose personal feelings to public scrutiny. This enabled them to explore new ground in terms of the content of their work but they could only do so because of the strength of their personal and theatrical relationship. At the same time, it became very clear that their relationship with audiences was essential to the development of their work, less in terms of specific feedback from audience members than because the performance environment provokes a special kind of experiencing for the performers. It is almost as if they split themselves in two and become, simultaneously, the actor on stage living the experience of the story and the observer in the auditorium experiencing the response.

At the beginning of my observation, thinking of Gecko as a physical theatre company, I expected that I would see a great deal of physical improvisation and I was surprised by how much time, relatively speaking, was spent talking rather than 'doing'. Perhaps my most important discovery is that I have come to understand that, for Gecko, the line between rehearsal and performance is a blurred one. It is in performance, as performers, that they make many of their most important discoveries and decisions.

Chronology of productions

Taylor's Dummies (2002) for BAC's Octoberfest, then national and international tours.

The Race (2005–7), South Hill Park, Bracknell, then national and international tours.

The Arab and The Jew (2007–8), The Pleasance, Edinburgh Fringe Festival, then for London International Mime Festival at the Lyric Theatre, Hammersmith, then national and international tours Autumn 2007.

For further information about the company see http://geckotheatre.com.

Notes

1. Gecko, joint interview with the author, 8 July 2008.
2. Rachel Halliburton, 'A Different Perspective on the Art of the Stage', review of *Taylor's Dummies*, *London Evening Standard*, 14 November 2002.
3. Lynn Gardner, review of *The Race*, 1 February 2005, Guardian Unlimited, http://www.guardian.co.uk/stage/2005/feb/01/theatre.shopping (accessed 20 July 2009).
4. Gecko, *Gecko 2007: Creation and Participation*, p. 9, PDF file, www.fueltheatre.com (accessed 20 July 2009).
5. Gecko's fourth show in 2009–10 was to be an adaptation of a Gogol short story, *The Overcoat*.

6. Gecko, programme for work-in-progress performance, the Junction, Cambridge, June 2007.
7. Al Nedjari, interview with the author, 18 October 2007.
8. Gecko, joint interview with the author, 8 July 2008.
9. Amit Lahav, interview with the author, 18 October 2007.
10. Ibid.
11. Nedjari, interview with the author, 18 October 2007.
12. Nedjari, interview with the author, 18 October 2007.
13. Lahav, interview with the author, 18 October 2007.
14. Nedjari, interview with the author, 18 October 2007.
15. Ibid.
16. Gecko, joint interview with the author, 8 July 2008.
17. Nedjari, interview with the author, 18 October 2007.
18. Lahav, interview with the author, 18 October 2007.
19. Ibid.
20. Gecko, Joint interview with the author, 8 July 2008.
21. Nedjari, interview with the author, 18 October 2007.
22. Gardner, L. 'The Battle to be Brothers', *Guardian*, 22 January 2008, http://www.guardian.co.uk/stage/2008/jan/22/theatre1 (accessed 20 July 2009).
23. Brian Logan, *Guardian*, 23 January 2008, http://www.guardian.co.uk/stage/2008/jan/23/theatre (accessed 20 July 2009).
24. Natascha Tripney, review of *The Arab and The Jew*, http://www.musicomh.com/theatre/the-arab_0108.htm accessed (20 July 2009).
25. Logan, op cit.

Bibliography

Bannerman, C., Sofaer, J. and Watt, J., eds. *Navigating the Unknown: The Creative Process in Contemporary Performing Arts*, Enfield: Middlesex University Press, 2006.

Barba, E. and Savarese, N. *A Dictionary of Theatre Anthropology: The Secret Art of the Performer*, London: Routledge, 1991.

Barthes, R. 'The Death of the Author', in R. Barthes, ed., *Image, Music, Text*, London: Fontana, 1977, pp. 142–8.

Bell, P. 'Dialogic Media Productions and Inter-media Exchange', *Journal of Dramatic Theory and Criticism* 14:2 (Fall 2000), pp. 41–56.

Bere, D. 'Underneath the Arches with Shunt', *Total Theatre Magazine* 13:4 (2001/2): (Winter) p. 8.

Bergson, H. *Matter and Memory*, trans. N. M. Paul and W. S. Palmer, New York: Zone Books, 1991.

Bouras, Z. 'Artist's Diary on Station House Opera's *The Other is You'*, *Total Theatre Magazine* 19:1 (Spring 2007): pp. 21–3.

Bourriaud, N. *Relational Aesthetics*, trans. Simon Pleasance and Fronza Woods with the participation of Mathieu Copeland, Dijon: Presses du Réel, 2002.

Brook, P. *The Shifting Point: Theatre, Film, Opera 1946–1987*, New York: Harper & Row, 1989.

Callery, D. *Through the Body: A Practical Guide to Physical Theatre*, London and New York: Routledge, 2001.

Chamberlain, F. and Yarrow R. *Jacques Lecoq and the British Theatre*, London and New York: Routledge, 2002.

Claxton, G. 'Creative Glide Space', in C. Bannerman, J. Sofaer and J. Watt, eds, *Navigating the Unknown: The Creative Process in Contemporary Performing Arts*, Enfield: Middlesex University Press, 2006, pp. 58–69.

Coyle, R. 'The Genesis of Virtual Reality', in *Future Visions: New Technologies of the screen*, ed. Philip Hayworth and Tana Wollen, London: British Film Institute, 1993, pp. 148–65.

Craig, S., ed. *Dreams and Deconstructions: Alternative Theatre in Britain*, Derbyshire: Amber Lane Press, 1980.

Darwin, C. *The Origin of Species by Means of Natural Selection*, London: Penguin Books, 1985.

Davies, A. *Other Theatres: The Development of Alternative and Experimental Theatre in Britain*, London: Macmillan Education, 1987.

Deleuze, G. *Bergsonism*, trans. H. Tomlinson and B. Habberjam, New York: Zone Books, 1988.

DiCenzo, M. *The Politics of Alternative Theatre in Britain 1968–1990*, Cambridge: Cambridge University Press, 1996.

Dostoevsky, F. *The Brothers Karamavoz*, trans. Richard Pevear and Larissa Volokhonsky, London: Vintage Books, 2004.

Elsom, J. 'People Show', in M. Banham (ed.), *The Cambridge Guide to Theatre*, Cambridge: Cambridge University Press, 1995, pp. 844–944.

Etchells, T. *Certain Fragments: Contemporary Performance and Forced Entertainment*, London and New York: Routledge, 1999.

Eyre, R. and Wright, N. *Changing Stages: A View of British Theatre in the Twentieth Century*, London: Bloomsbury, 2000.

Felman, S. and Laub, D. *Testimony: Crises of Witnessing in Literature, Psychoanalysis and History*, London: Routledge, 1992.

Glass, D. *Creative Practice: A Guide to Creativity in Development*, VBNK, Phnom Penh and London: David Glass Ensemble, 2003.

Gleick, J. *Chaos: The Amazing Science of the Unpredictable*, London: Vintage, 1998.

Goldberg, R. *Performance Art: From Futurism to the Present*, London: Thames and Hudson, 2001.

Goodman, L. *Contemporary Feminist Theatres: To Each Her Own*, London: Routledge, 1993.

Gottlieb, V. and Chambers, C., eds, *Theatre in a Cool Climate*, Oxford: Amber Lane Press, 1999.

Govan, E., Nicholson, H. and Normington, K. *Making a Performance: Devising Histories and Contemporary Practices*, London: Routledge, 2007.

Grant, B. 'Film Authorship and Collaboration' in R. Allen and M. Smith (eds.), *Film Theory and Philosophy*, Oxford, Oxford University Press, 1997, pp. 149–73.

Graver, D. *The Aesthetics of Disturbance: Anti-art in Avant-Garde Drama*, Ann Arbor, MI: University of Michigan Press, 1995.

Hanna, G. *Monstrous Regiment: Four Plays and a Collective Celebration*, London: Nick Hern, 1991.

Harvie, J. and Lavender, A., eds, *Making Contemporary Theatre: International Rehearsal Processes*, Manchester: Manchester University Press, 2010.

Heddon, D. and Milling, J. *Devising Performance: A Critical History*, London: Palgrave Macmillan, 2006.

Hewison, R. *Too Much: Art and Society in the Sixties 1960–75*, London: Methuen, 1986.

Hulton, P. *Interview with Mark Long*, Dartington Theatre Papers, 1981–82.

Jones, A. 'Survey', in T. Warr, ed., *The Artist's Body: Themes and Movements*, London: Phaidon, 2002, pp. 16–48.

Kelly, A. 'Class of "76"', in A. Heathfield, ed., *Small Acts: Performance, the Millennium and the Marking of Time*, London: Black Dog Publishing, 2000, pp. 45–51.

Kelly, J. 'Pop Music and Multimedia: Presence, Intermediality and Virtual Representation in Pop-music Performance', in J. Sexton, ed., *Music, Sound and Multimedia: From the Live to the Virtual (Music and the Moving Image)*, Edinburgh: Edinburgh University Press, 2007, pp. 105–21.

Kershaw, B. *The Politics of Performance: Radical Theatre as Cultural Intervention*, London: Routledge, 1992.

—— *The Radical in Performance: From Brecht to Baudrillard*, London: Routledge, 1999.

Kirby, M. 'Happenings: An Introduction', in M. R. Sandford, ed., *Happenings and Other Acts*, London and New York: Routledge, 1995, pp. 1–28.

—— 'On Acting and Not-Acting', in Philip B. Zarrilli, ed., *Acting (Re)Considered: A Theoretical and Practical Guide*, London: Routledge, 2002, pp. 40–52.

Kirby Nes, V. 'The Creation and Development of *People Show #52*', *The Drama Review* 18:2 (1974), pp. 48–66.

Lamden, G. *Devising: A Handbook for Drama and Theatre Students*, London: Hodder and Stoughton, 2000.

Lavender, A. 'Turns and Transformations', in V. Gottlieb and C. Chambers, eds, *Theatre in a Cool Climate*, Oxford: Amber Lane Press, 1999, pp. 179–90.

Lecoq, J. with Carasso, J. G. and Lallias, J. C. *The Moving Body: Teaching Creative Theatre*, trans. D. Bradby, New York: Routledge, 2001.

Lehmann, H.-T. *Postdramatic Theatre*, London: Routledge, 2006.

Long, M. 'About the People Show', *The Drama Review* 15:4 (1971), pp. 47–57.

—— interviewed by Peter Hulton in *Arts Archives, Theatre Papers, The Fourth Series 1983–4*, Exeter: Arts Documentation Unit.

Mendus, C. 'Competitive Co-operation: Playing with Theatre de Complicité', *New Theatre Quarterly* 22:3 (August 2006), pp. 257–67.

Mitchell, K. 'Liberate, Don't Refrigerate', in V. Gottlieb and C. Chambers, eds, *Theatre in a Cool Climate*, Oxford: Amber Lane Press, 1999, pp. 69–78.

Murray, S. *Jacques Lecoq*, London: Routledge, 2003.

Murray, S. and Keefe, J., eds, *Physical Theatres: A Critical Introduction*, London: Routledge, 2007.

Nicholson, H. *Applied Drama: The Gift of Theatre*, London: Palgrave Macmillan, 2005.

Nuttall, J. *Performance Art Memoirs. Volume 1*, London: John Calder, 1979.

Oddey, A. *Devising Theatre: A Practical and Theoretical Handbook*, London: Routledge, 1996.

Phelan, P. *Unmarked: The Politics of Performance*, London: Routledge, 1992.

Race, D., ed. *Leadership and Change in Human Services: Selected Readings from Wolf Wolfensberger*, London: Routledge, 2003.

Rees, R. *Fringe First: Pioneers of Fringe Theatre on Record*, London, Oberon Books, 1992.

Reid, T. 'Deformities of the Frame: The Theatre of Anthony Neilson', *Contemporary Theatre Review* 17:4 (2007), pp. 487–98.

Sanchez-Colberg, A. 'Altered States and Subliminal Spaces: Charting the Road Towards a Physical Theatre', *Performance Research* 1:2 (1996), pp. 40–56.

Sardar, Z. and Abrams, I. *Introducing Chaos*, Royston: Icon Books, 2004.

Shevtsova, M. *Dodin and the Maly Drama Theatre: Process to Performance*, New York: Routledge, 2004.

Sobieski, L. 'Breaking the Boundaries: The People Show, Lumière & Son and Hesitate and Demonstrate', in T. Shanks, ed., *Contemporary British Theatre*, London, Macmillan, 1994, pp. 89–106.

Walsh, Enda and theatre O. *Delirium: After The Brothers Karamavoz*, London: Nick Hern, 2008.

Warr, T., ed. *The Artist's Body: Themes and Movements*, London: Phaidon, 2002.

Williams, R. *Dostoevksy: Language, Faith and Fiction*, Texas: Continuum, 2008.

Index